Günter Gerngross • Herbert Puchta

PLAYWAY

1

TO ENGLISH

Story Cards

CAMBRIDGE
UNIVERSITY PRESS

Helbling

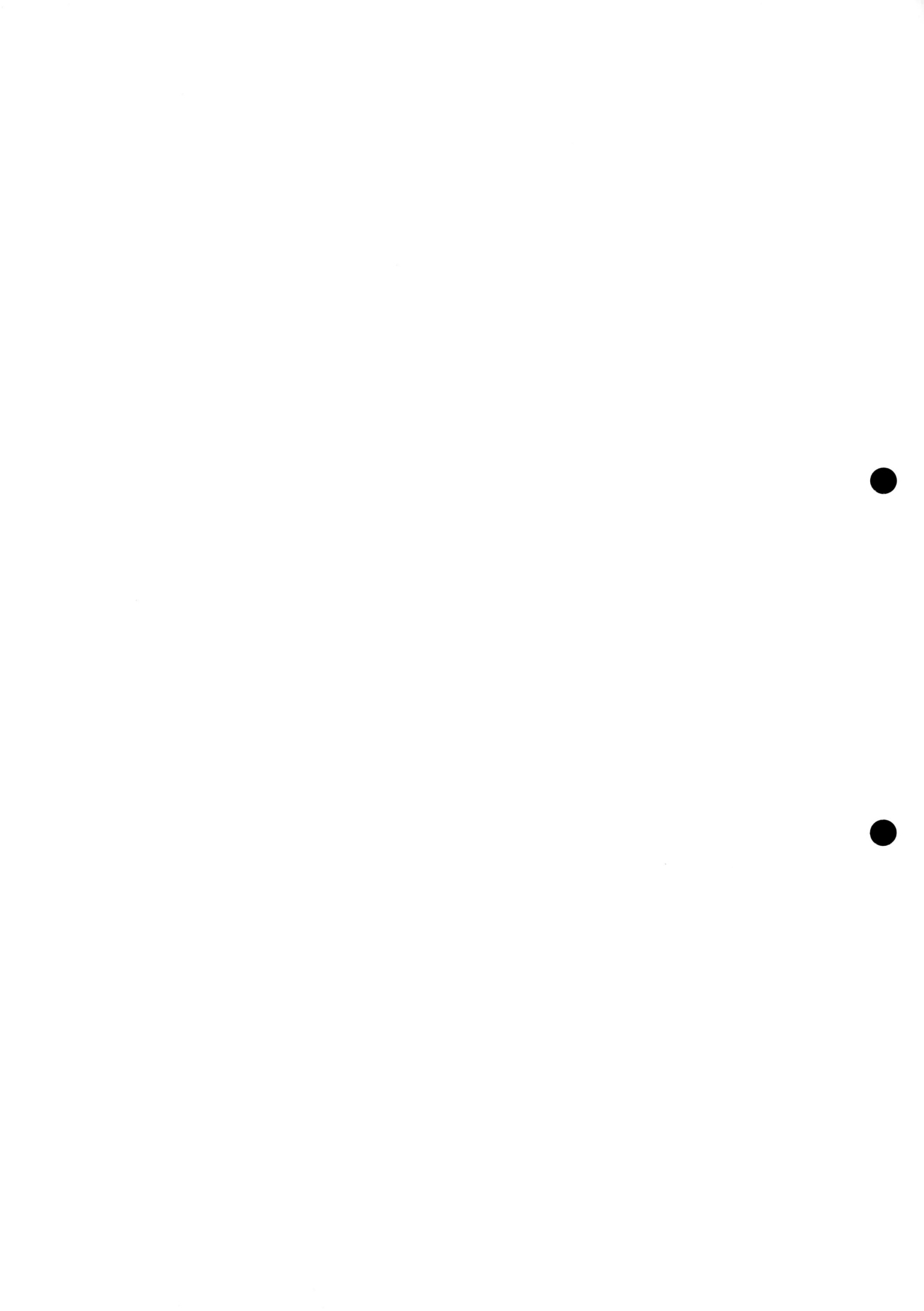

Günter Gerngross • Herbert Puchta

PLAYWAY 1
TO ENGLISH
Story Cards

for the reconstruction of cartoon stories

Illustrations by Svjetlan Junaković

ISBN 0521 656915

Layout by Gio Festin

© Cambridge University Press and Helbling, Rum/Innsbruck 1998

CAMBRIDGE
UNIVERSITY PRESS

Helbling

Linda and Benny are going shopping.

"Two apples, please."

Playway to English 1 • Story Cards • © Cambridge University Press and Helbling, Rum/Innsbruck 1998   FRUIT: Going shopping

"Here you are."

"Three bananas, please."

"Here you are."

Playway to English 1 • Story Cards • © Cambridge University Press and Helbling, Rum/Innsbruck 1998

"Four pears, please."

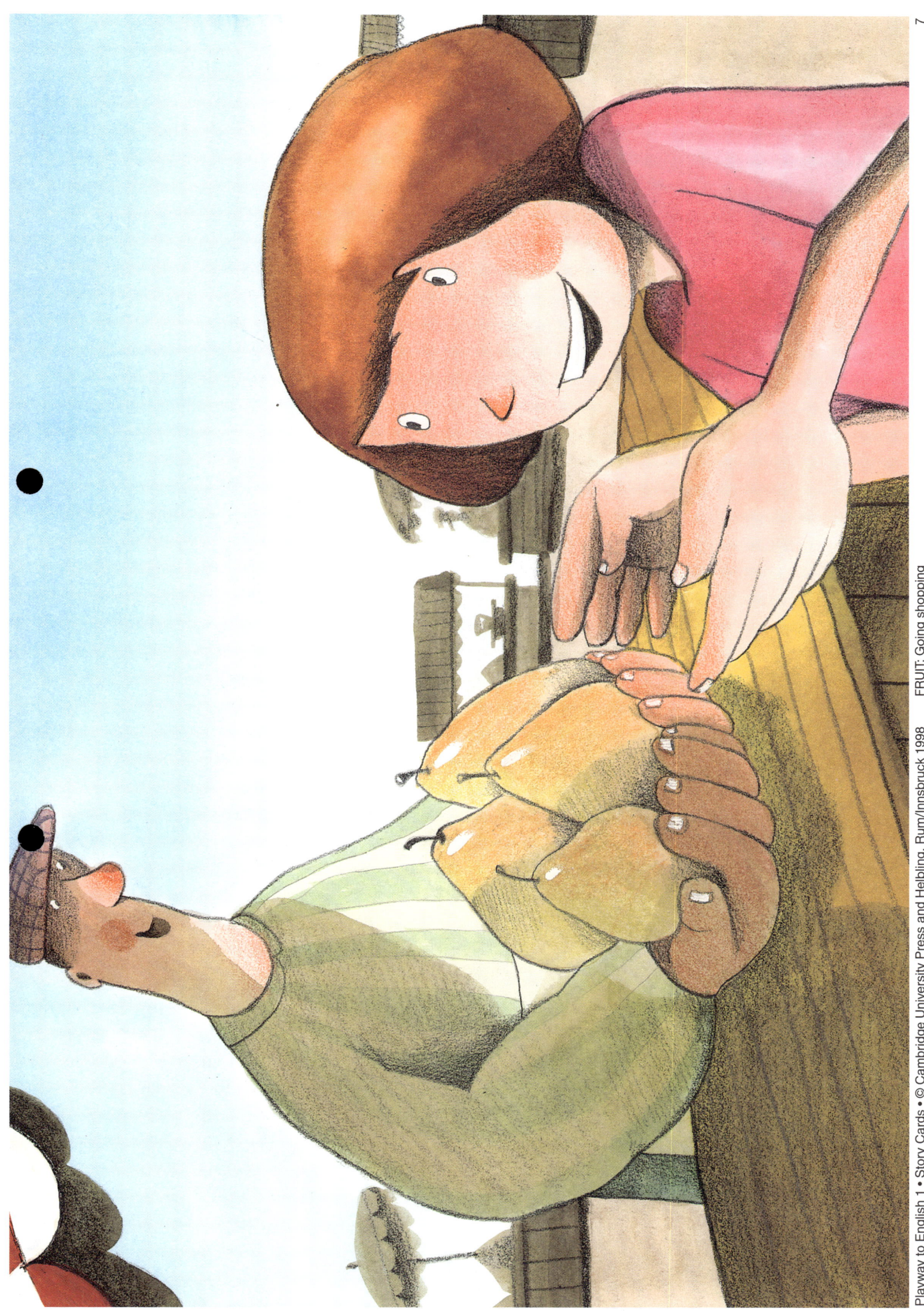

Playway to English 1 • Story Cards • © Cambridge University Press and Helbling, Rum/Innsbruck 1998

"Here you are."

"Have a plum."

"Yummy."

Linda and Benny are at home.

Oh, here's Max.

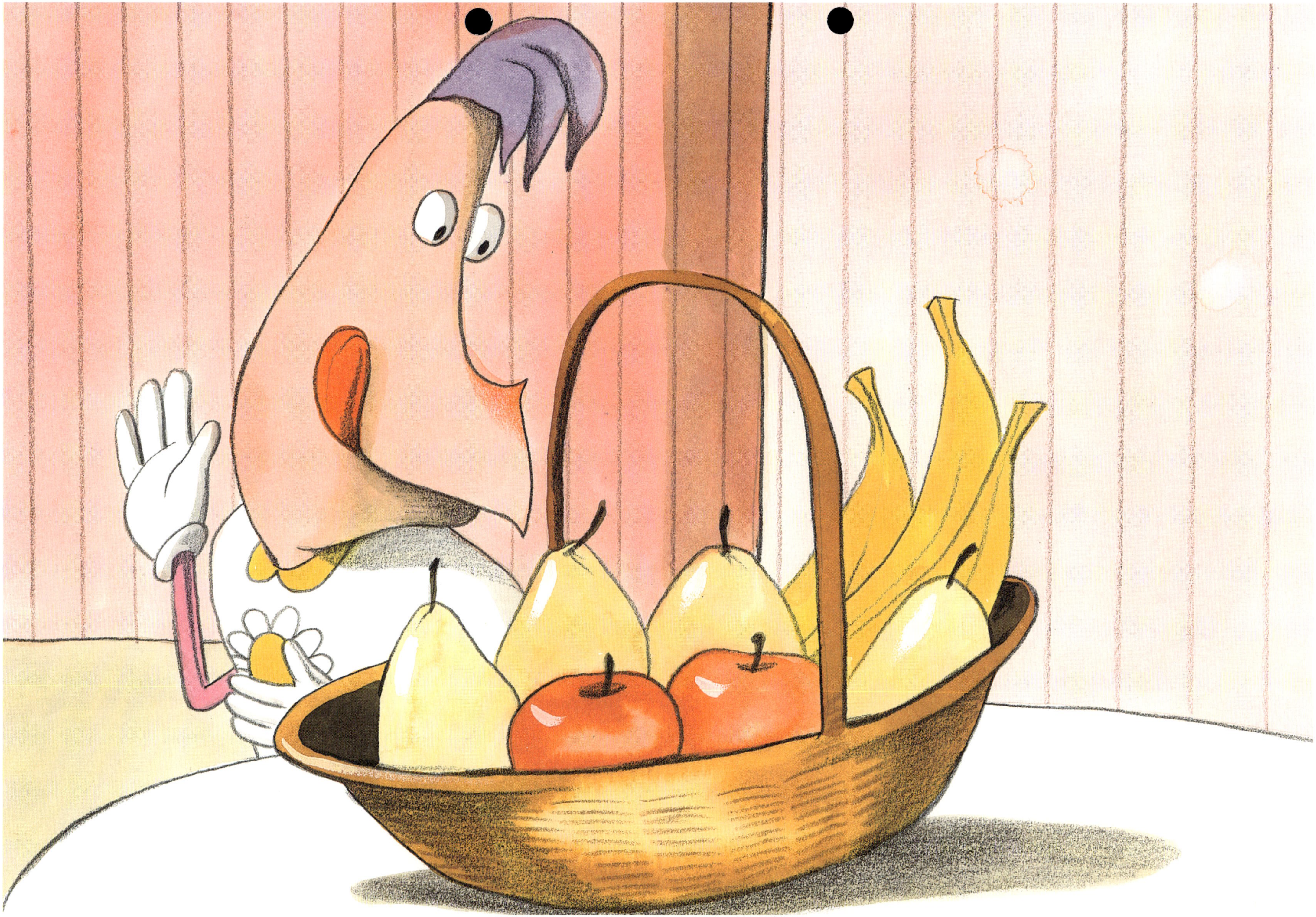

Playway to English 1 • Story Cards • © Cambridge University Press and Helbling, Rum/Innsbruck 1998

"Mmmmh."

So what's in the basket?

Two apples?

No.

Three bananas?

No. No.

Two pears?

No. No.

No. No. No.

No apples, no bananas, no pears.

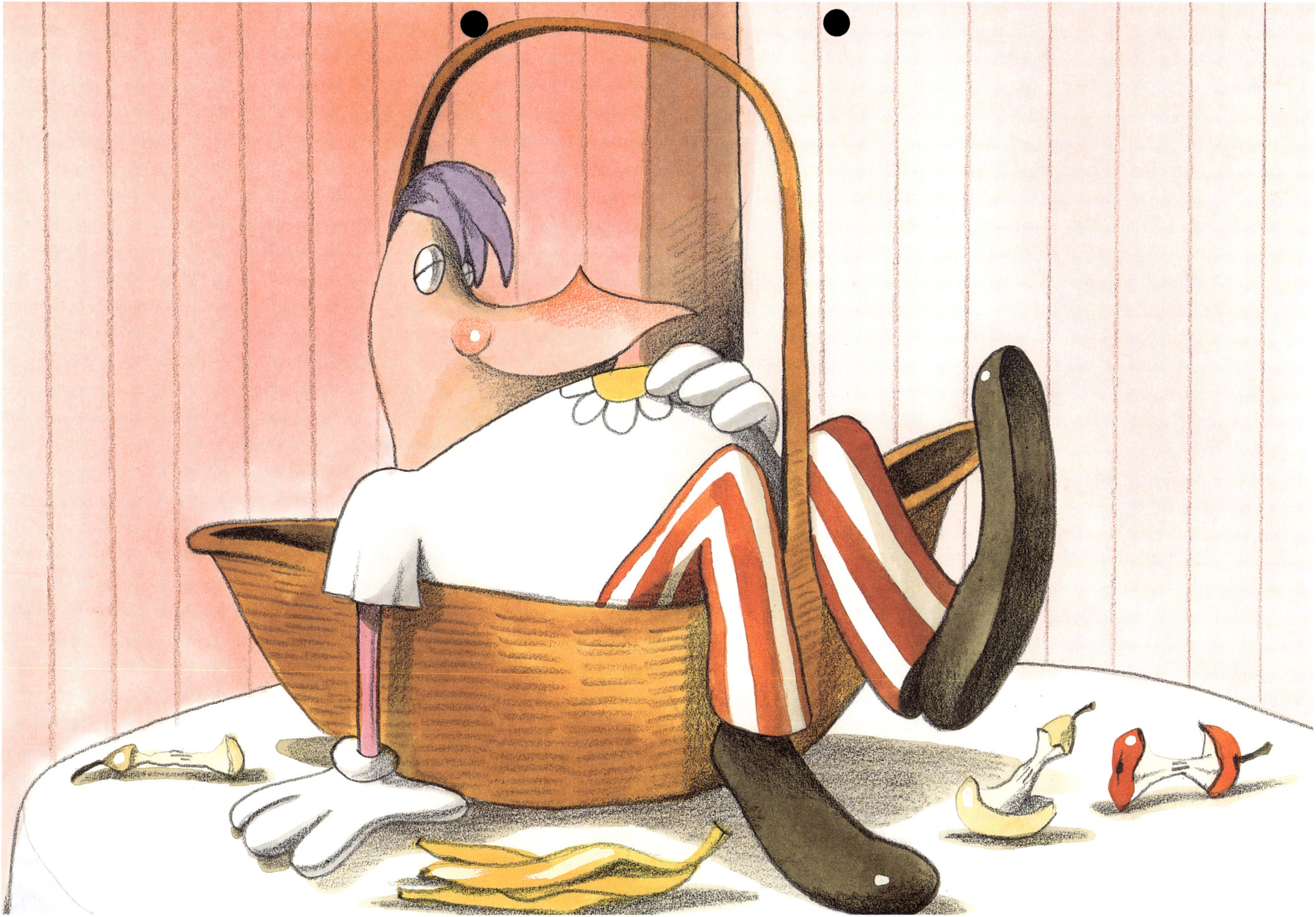

It's Max!

"Hello dog.
Squeak, squeak.
Let's play."

"No, go away.
Woof, woof."

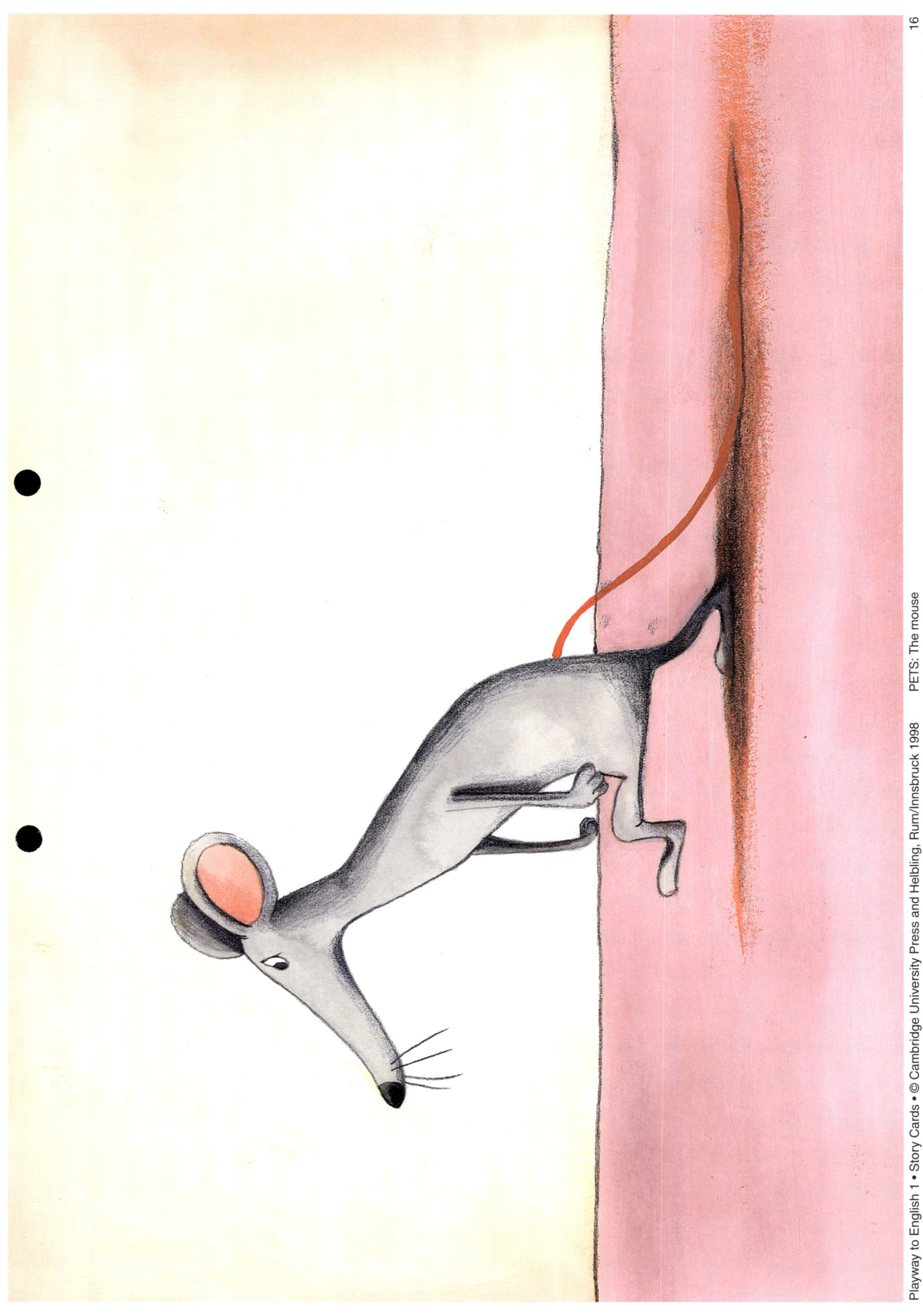

The mouse goes away.

"Hello cat.
Squeak, squeak.
Let's play."

"No, go away.
Meow!"

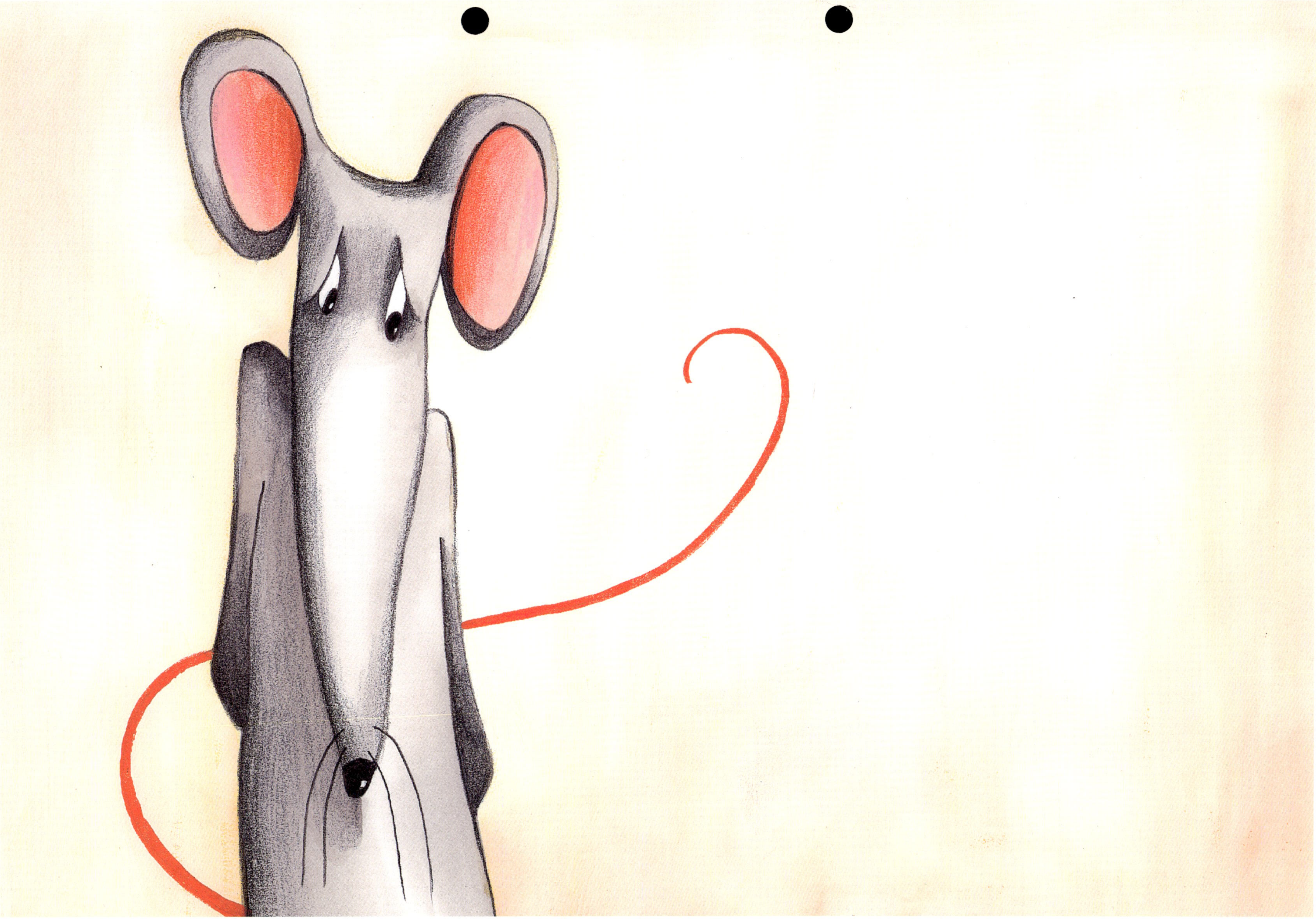

The mouse is sad.

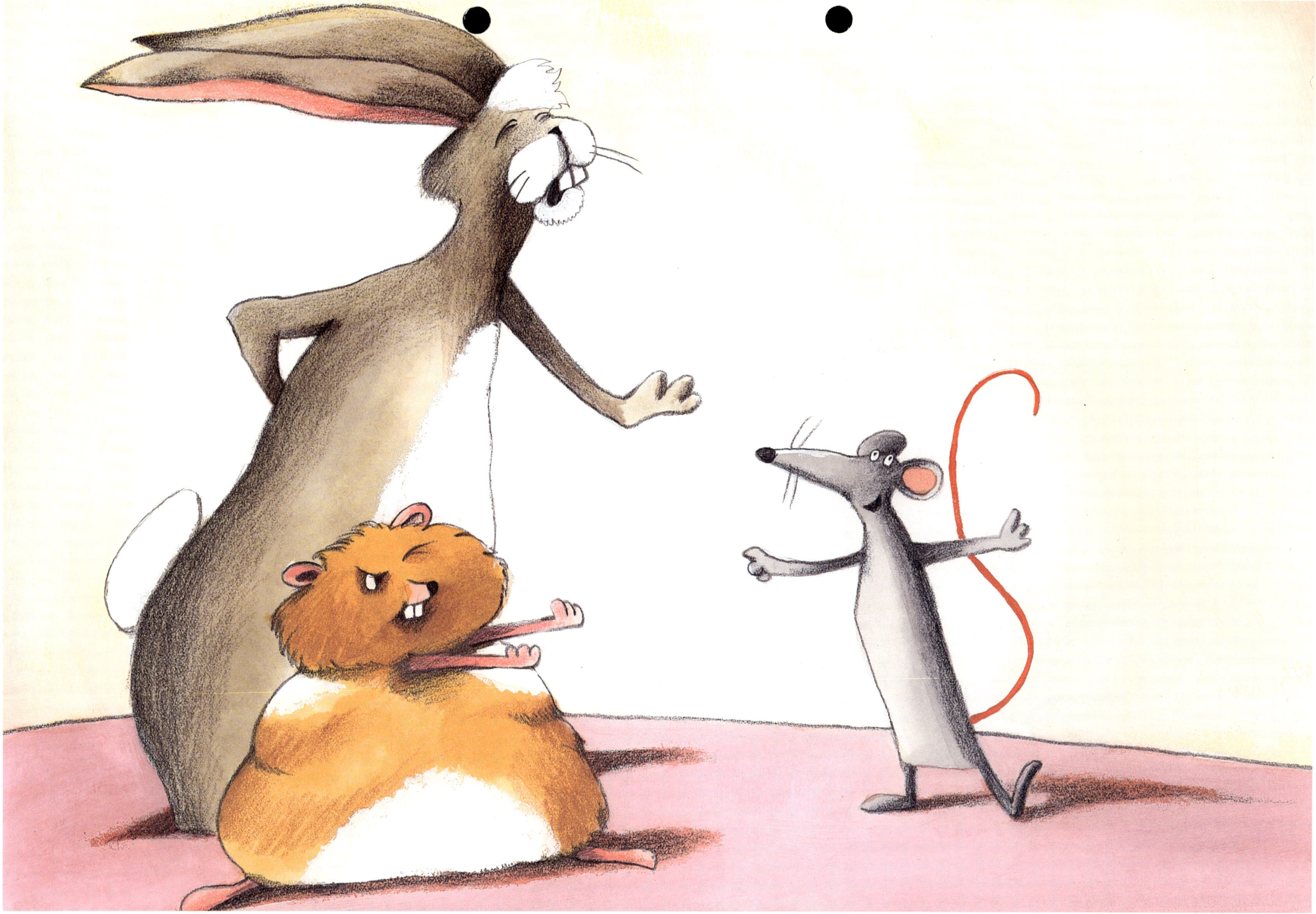

"Hello rabbit, hello hamster.
Squeak, squeak.
Let's play."

"No, go away."

The mouse is very sad.

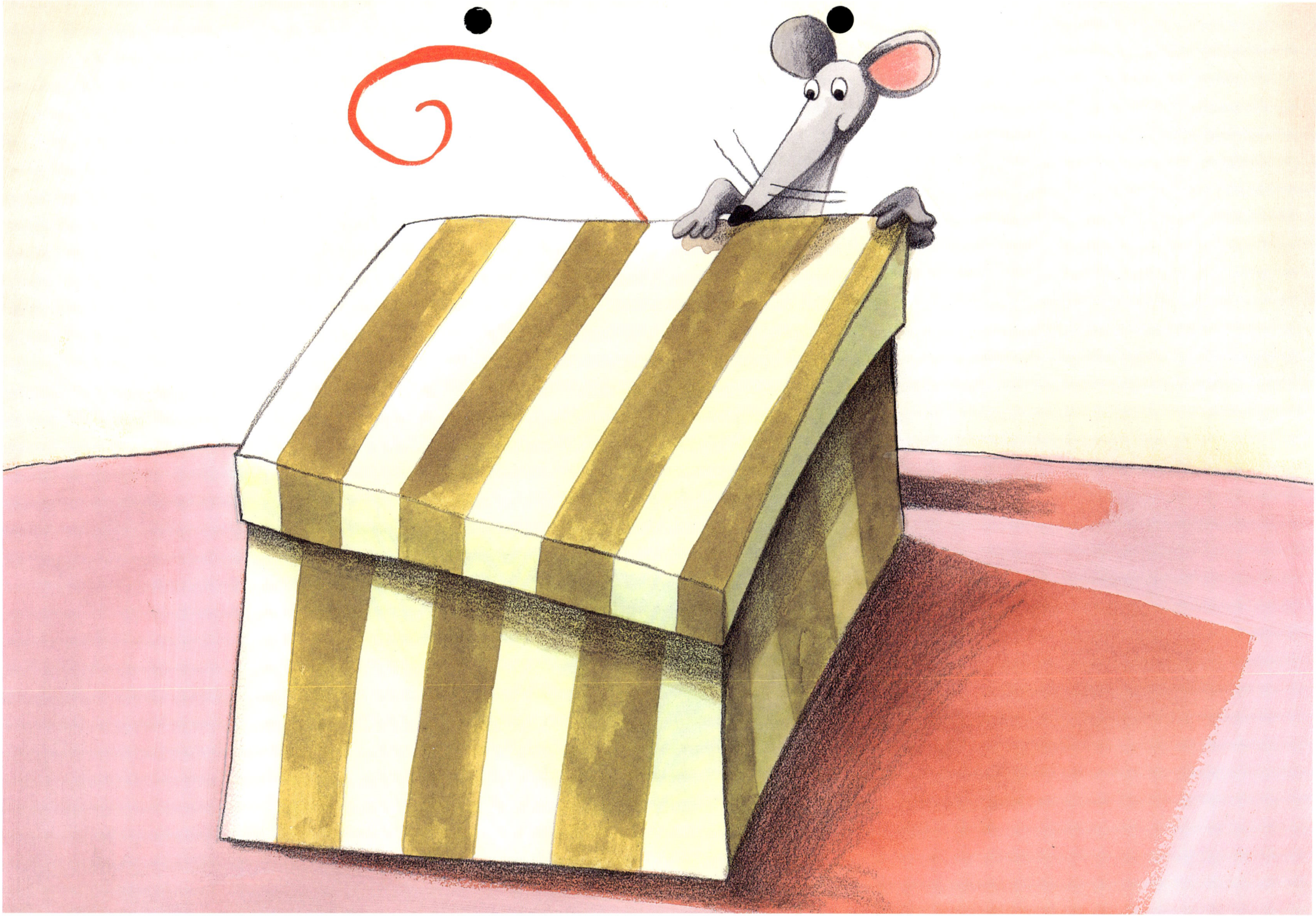

"Oh, what's this?"

"Wonderful."

"Abracadabra, one, two, three."

"Oooooh!"
"Woof, woof! Let's go to the show."
"Yes."

"A duck!"
"Super!"

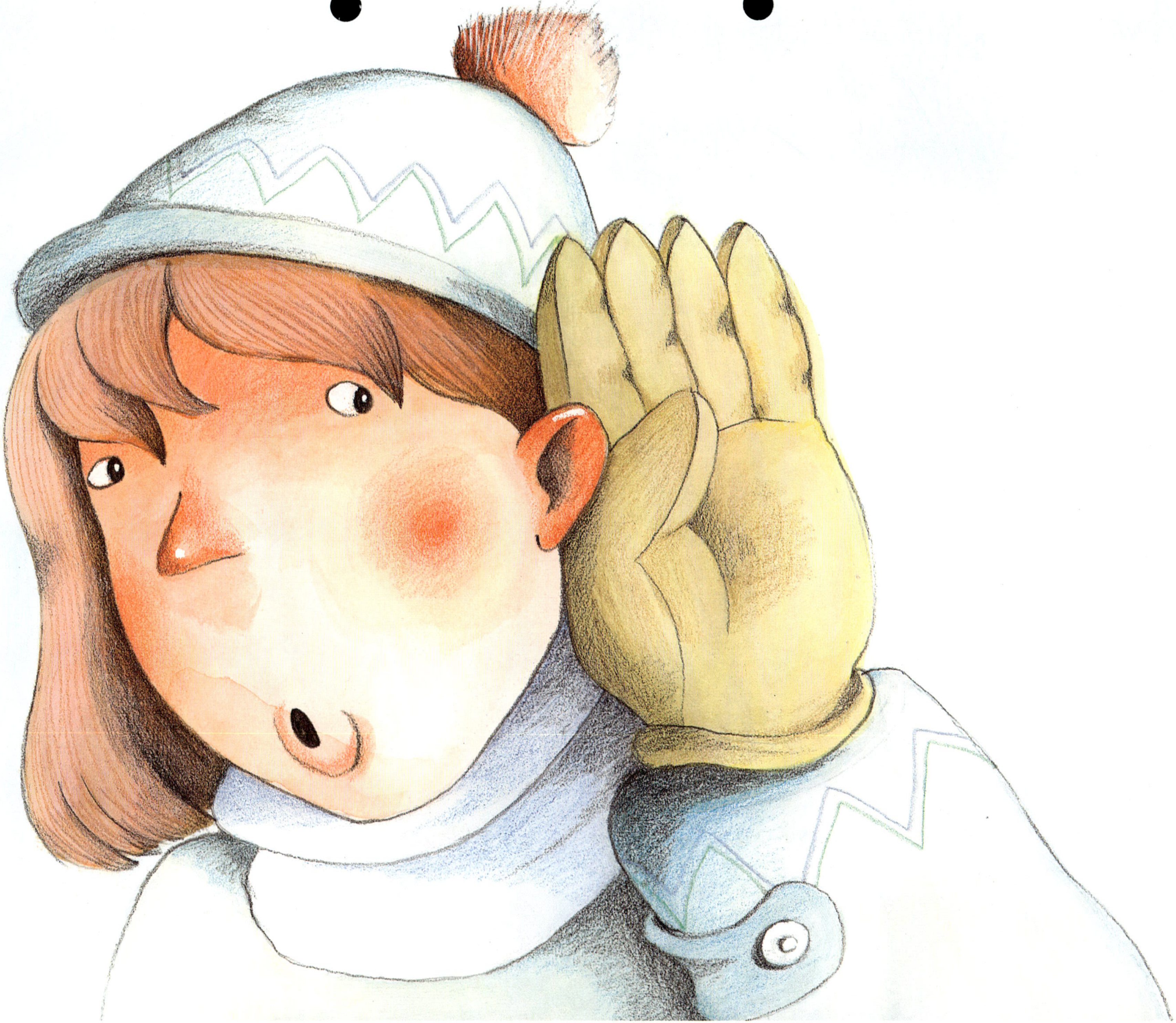

Listen.

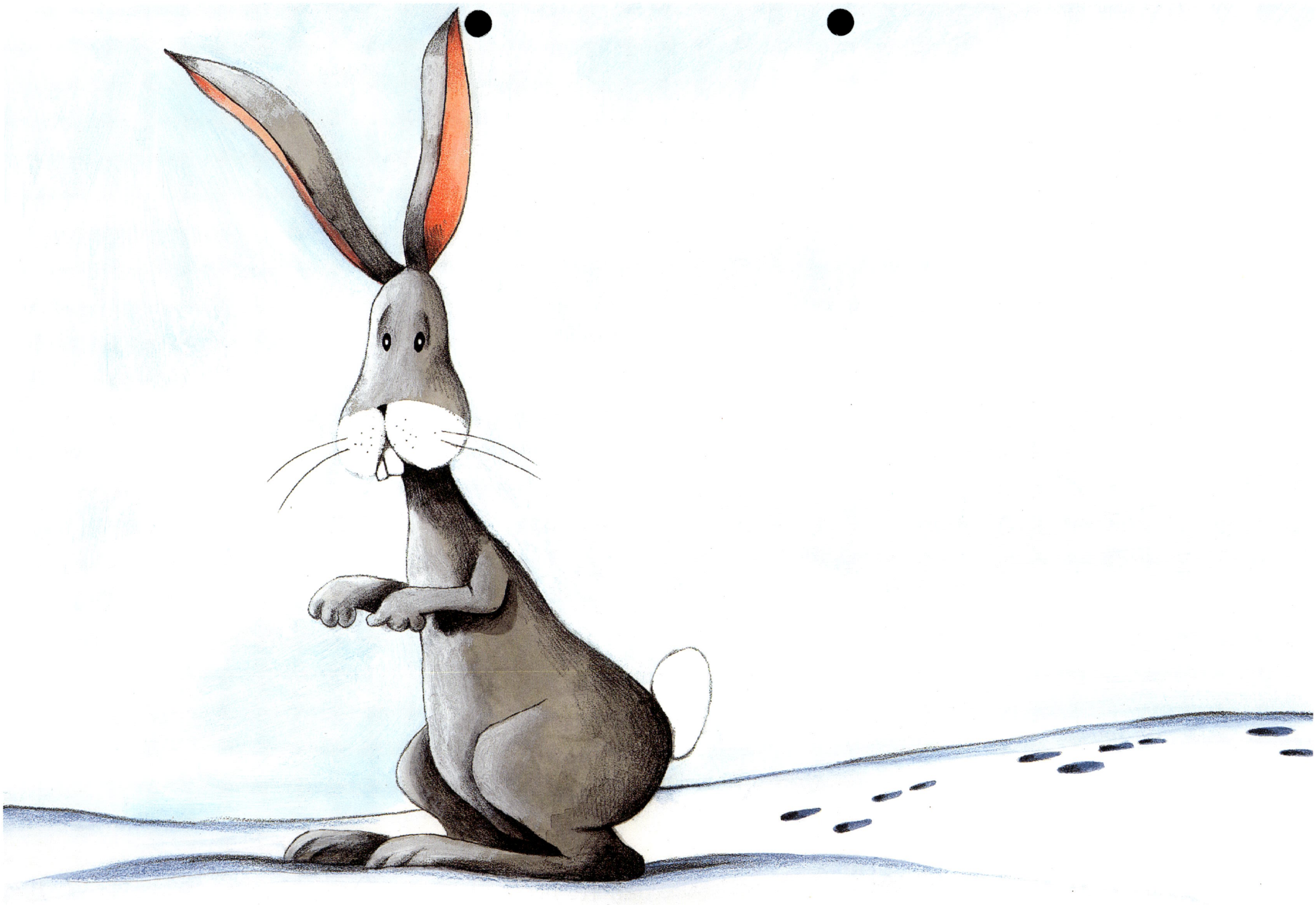

A rabbit.

●

●

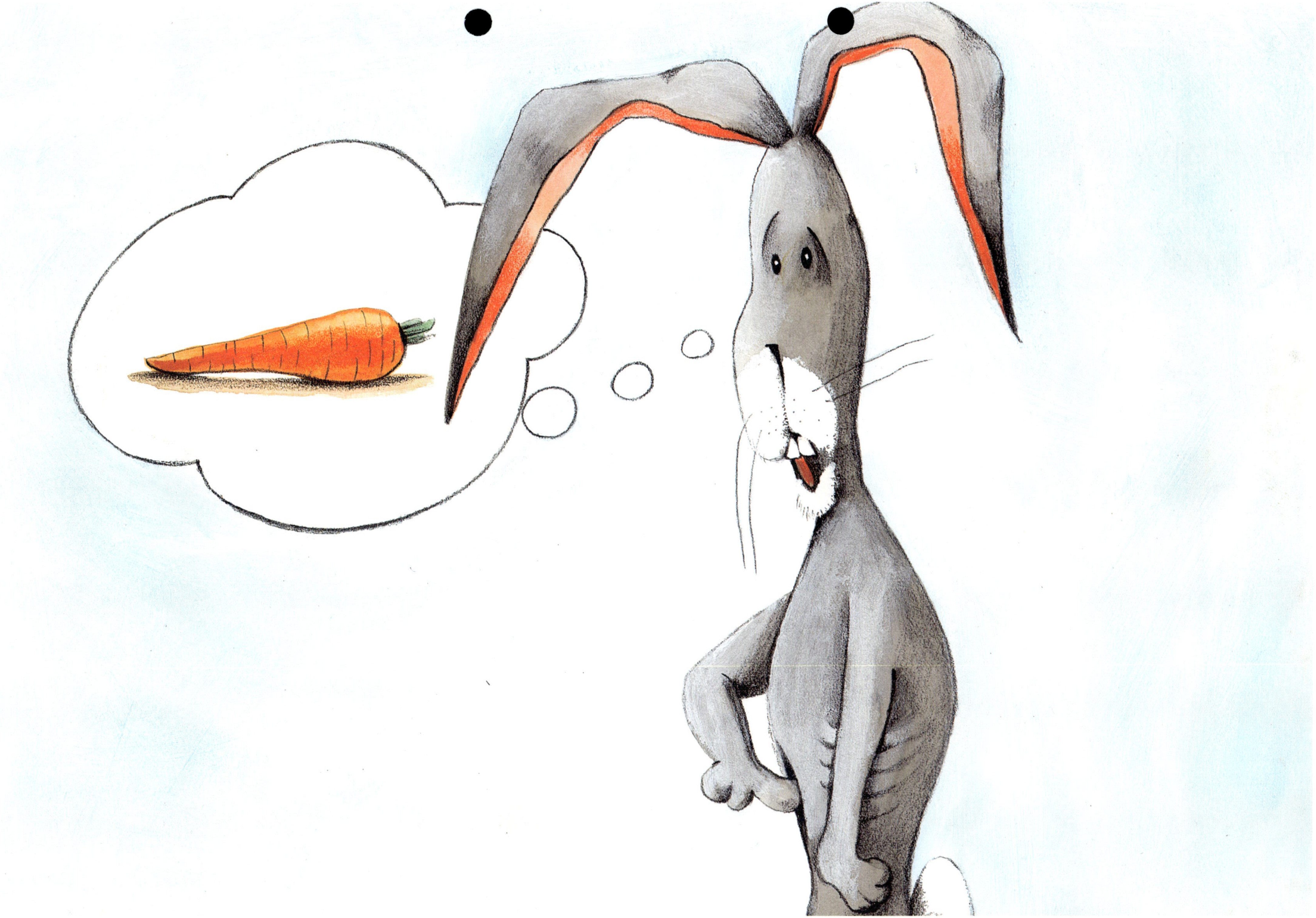

The rabbit is hungry.

What's this?

A snowman.

●

●

Playway to English 1 • Story Cards • © Cambridge University Press and Helbling, Rum/Innsbruck 1998   WINTER: The snowman

Playway to English 1 • Story Cards • © Cambridge University Press and Helbling, Rum/Innsbruck 1998

"Mmmmh! What a big nose!"

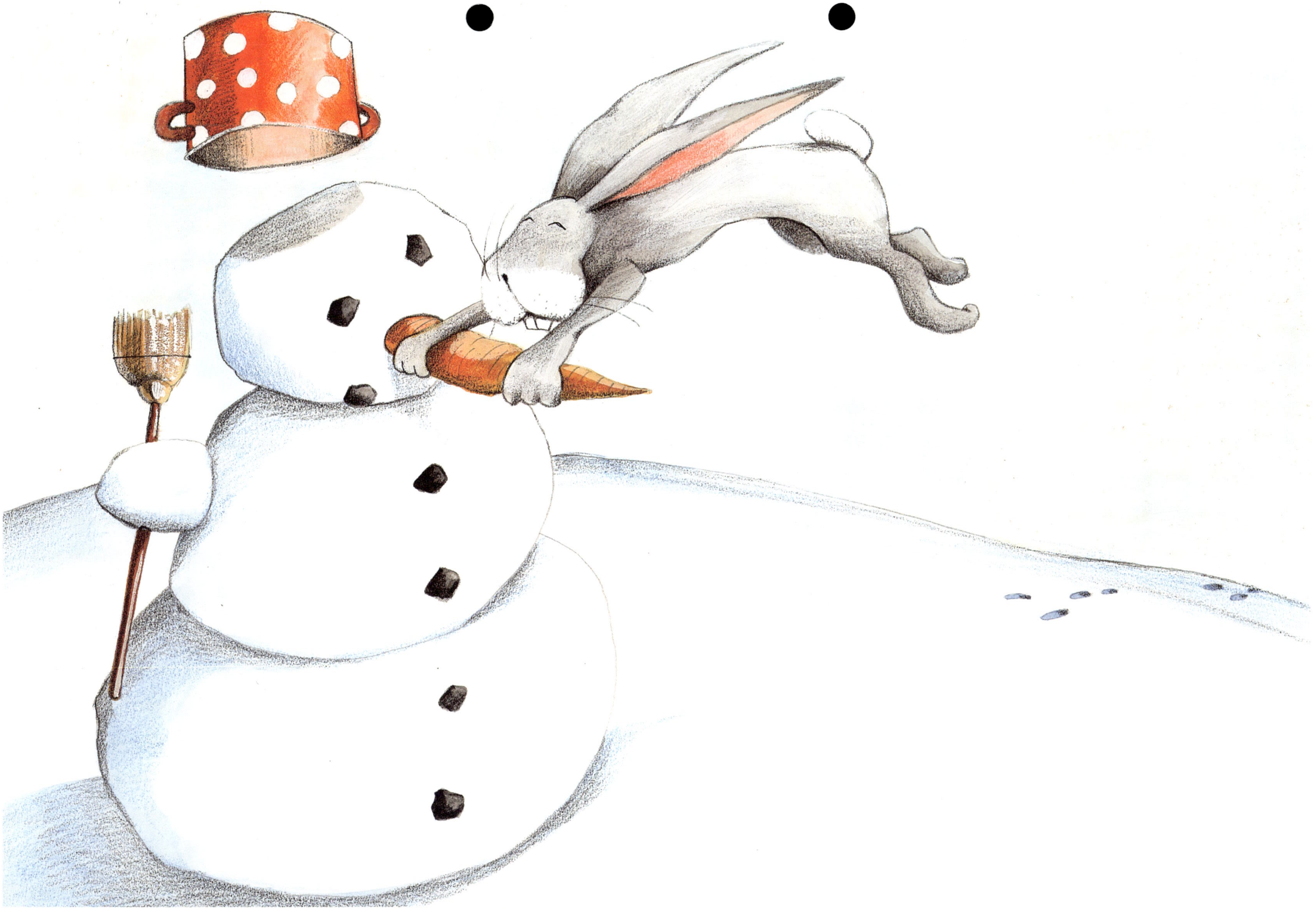

"Got it."

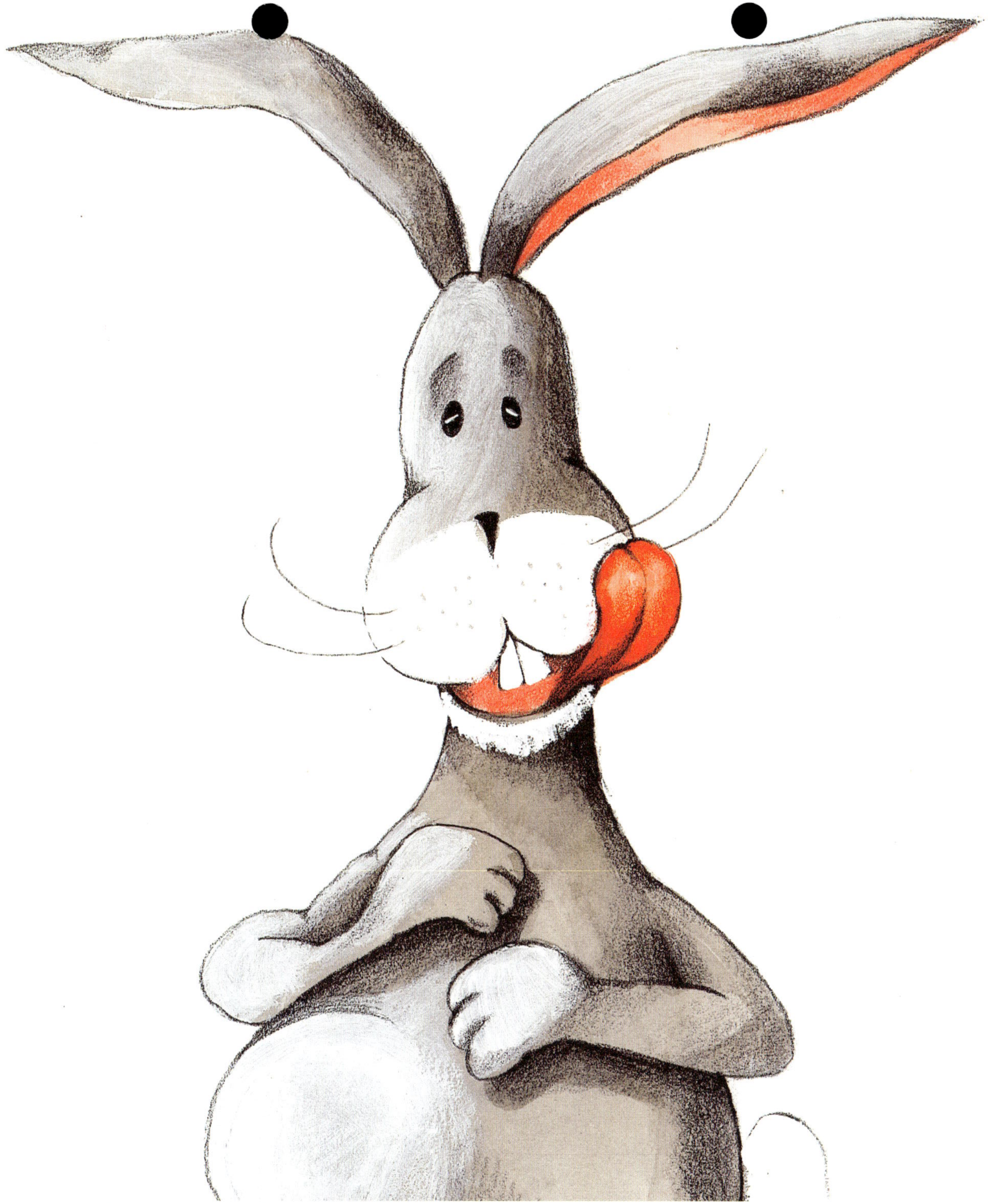

"Yummy."

The little seed is asleep.

Look at the clouds.

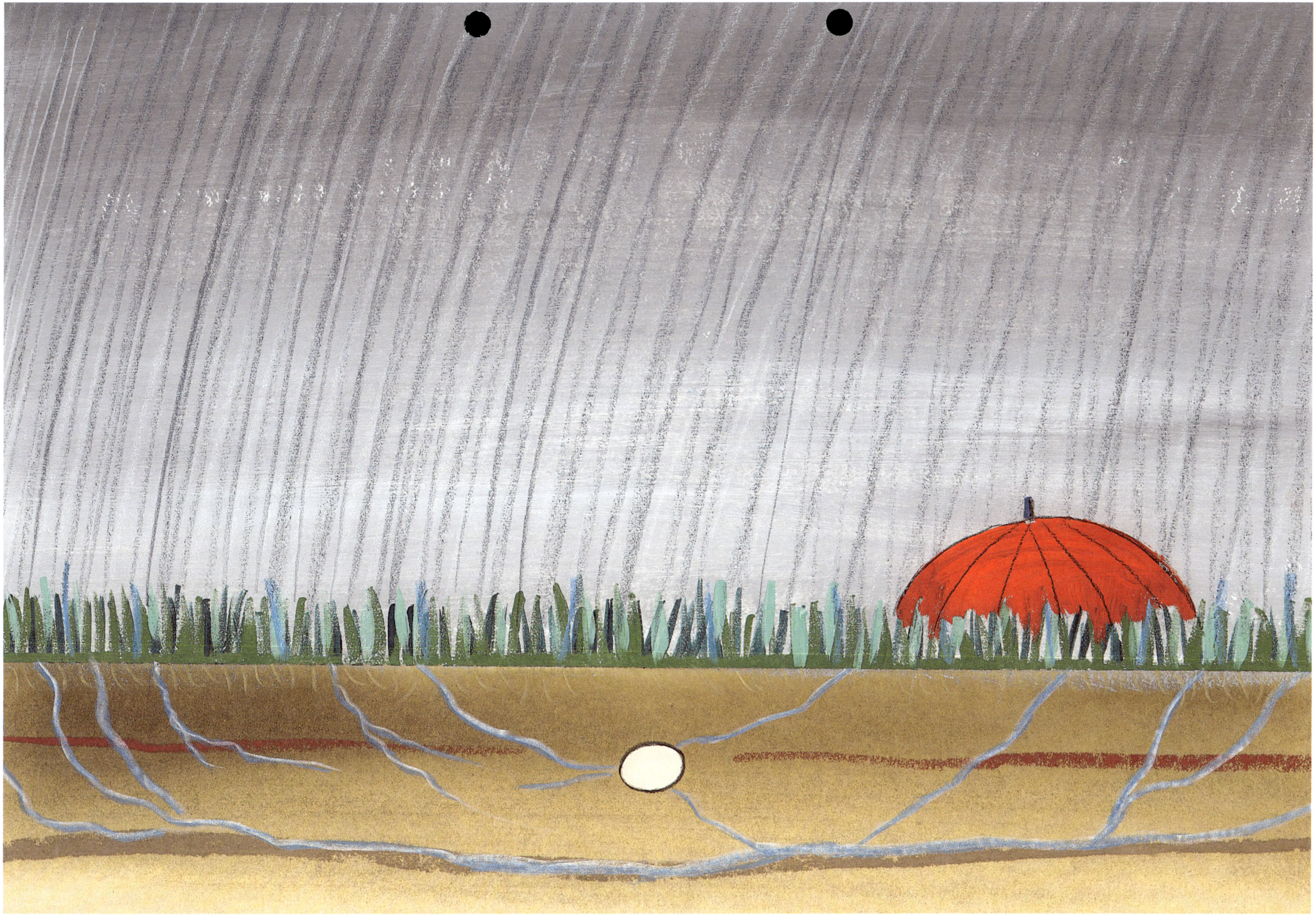

It's raining. It's raining and raining.

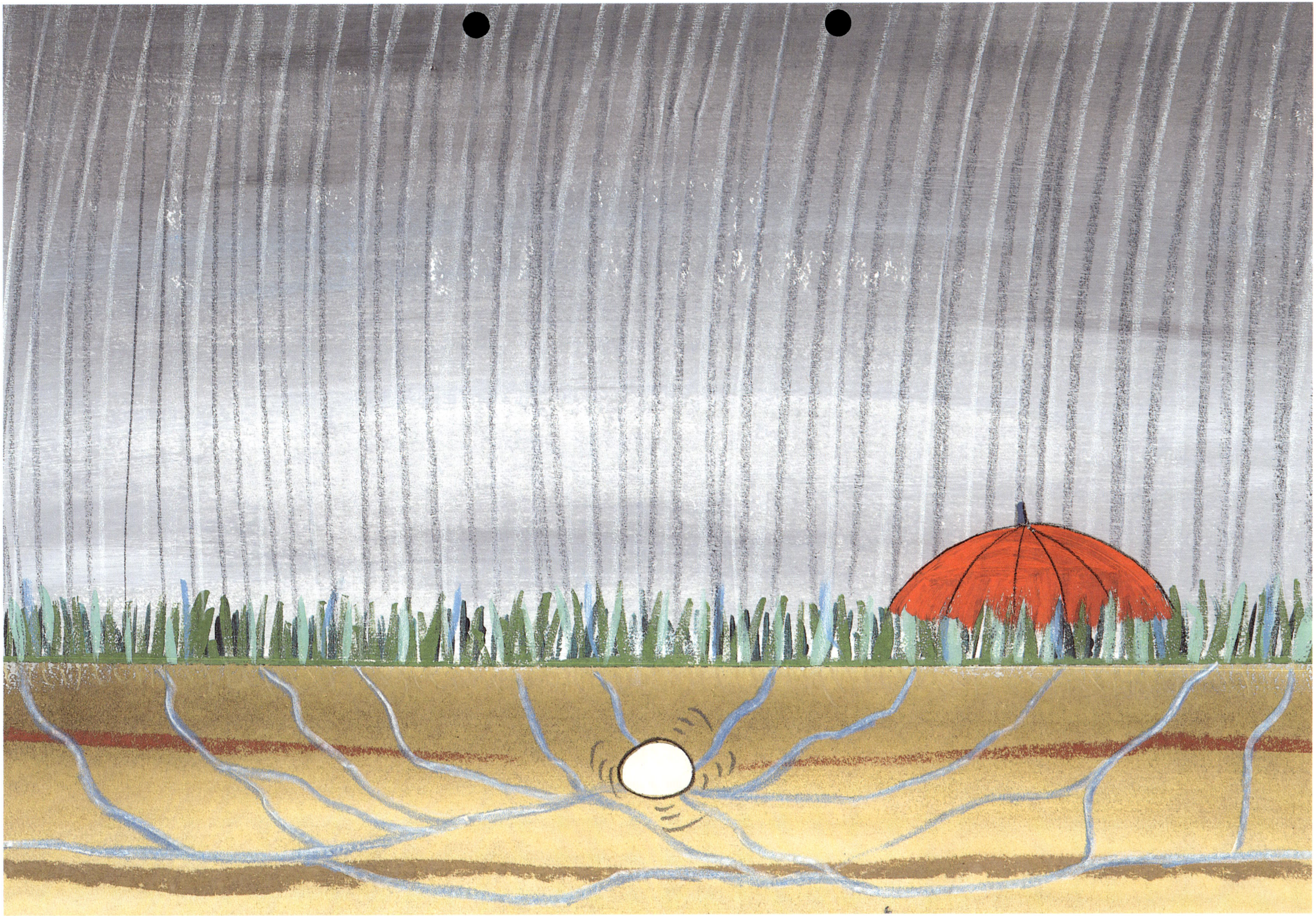

The little seed grows.

Playway to English 1 • Story Cards • © Cambridge University Press and Helbling, Rum/Innsbruck 1998

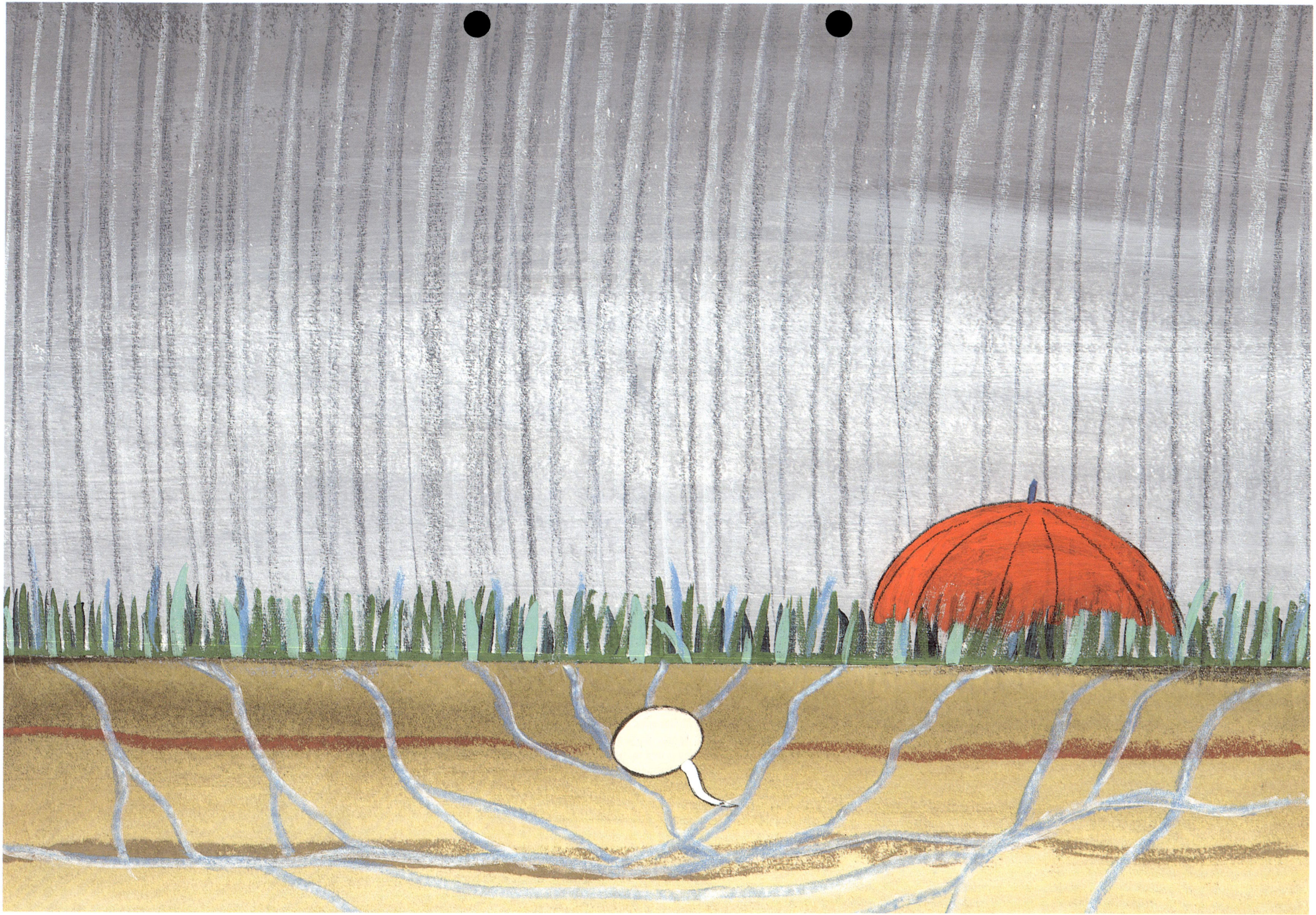

It grows and grows.

●

●

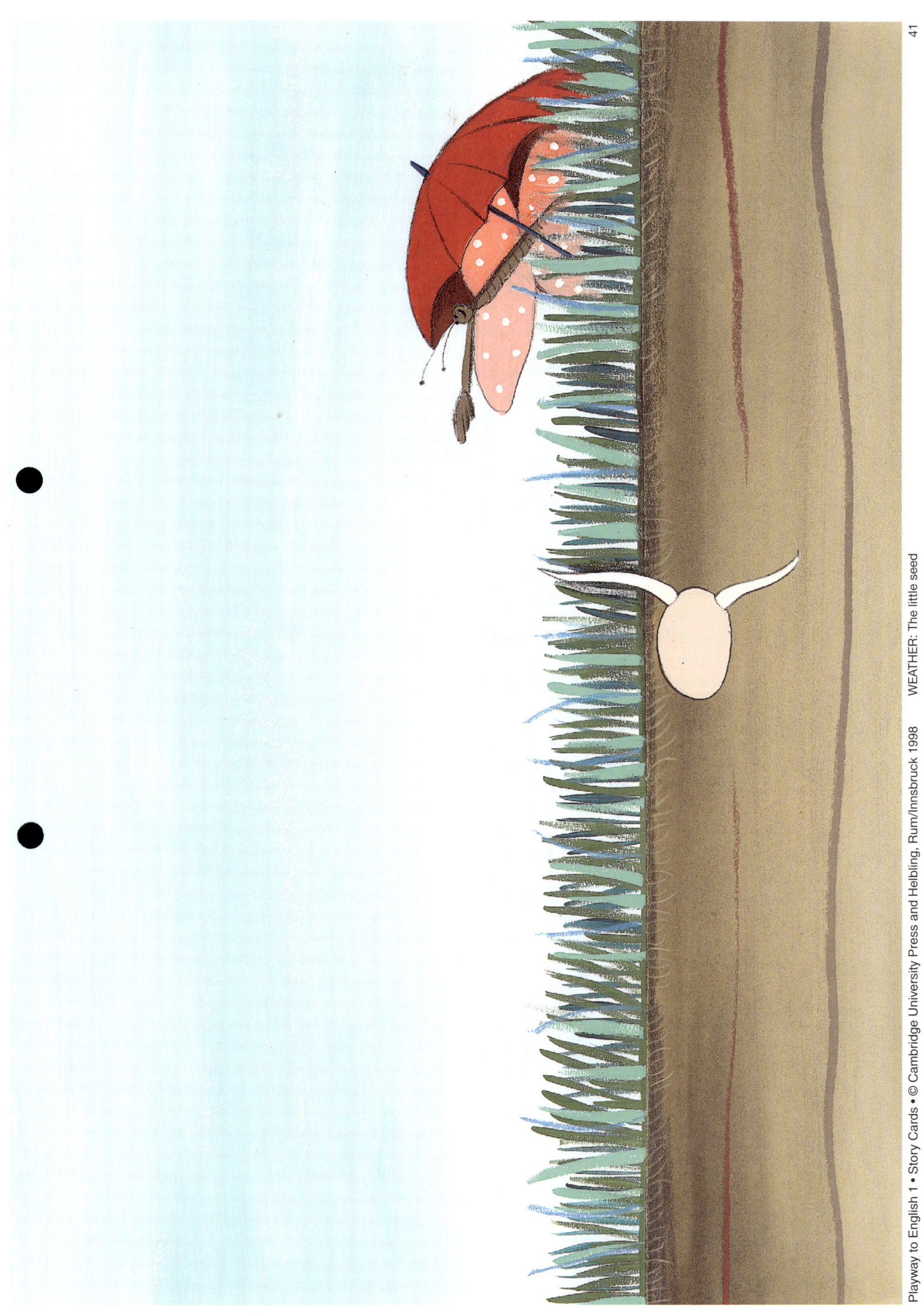

Playway to English 1 • Story Cards • © Cambridge University Press and Helbling, Rum/Innsbruck 1998

The rain stops.

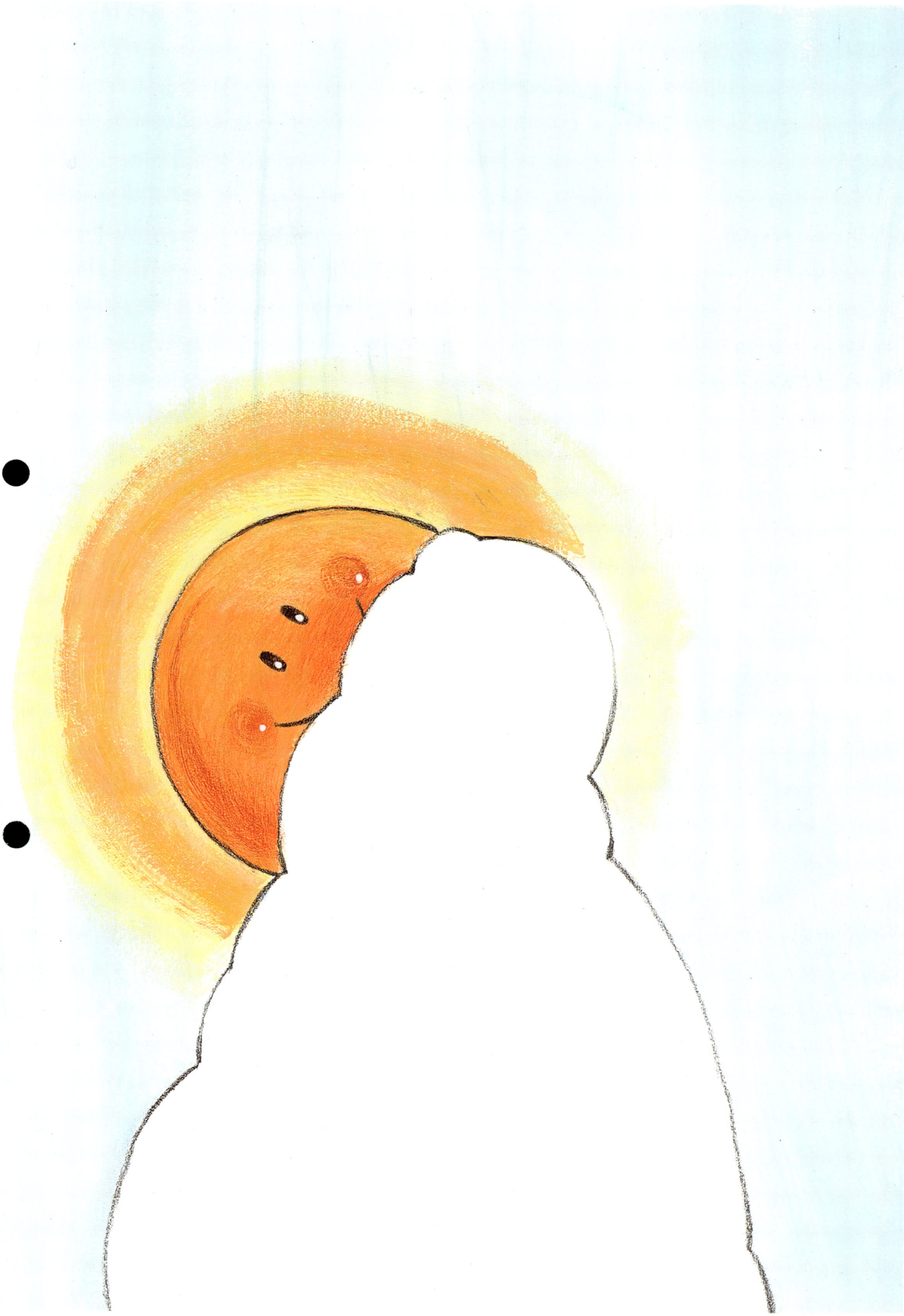

Look. Here comes the sun.

●

●

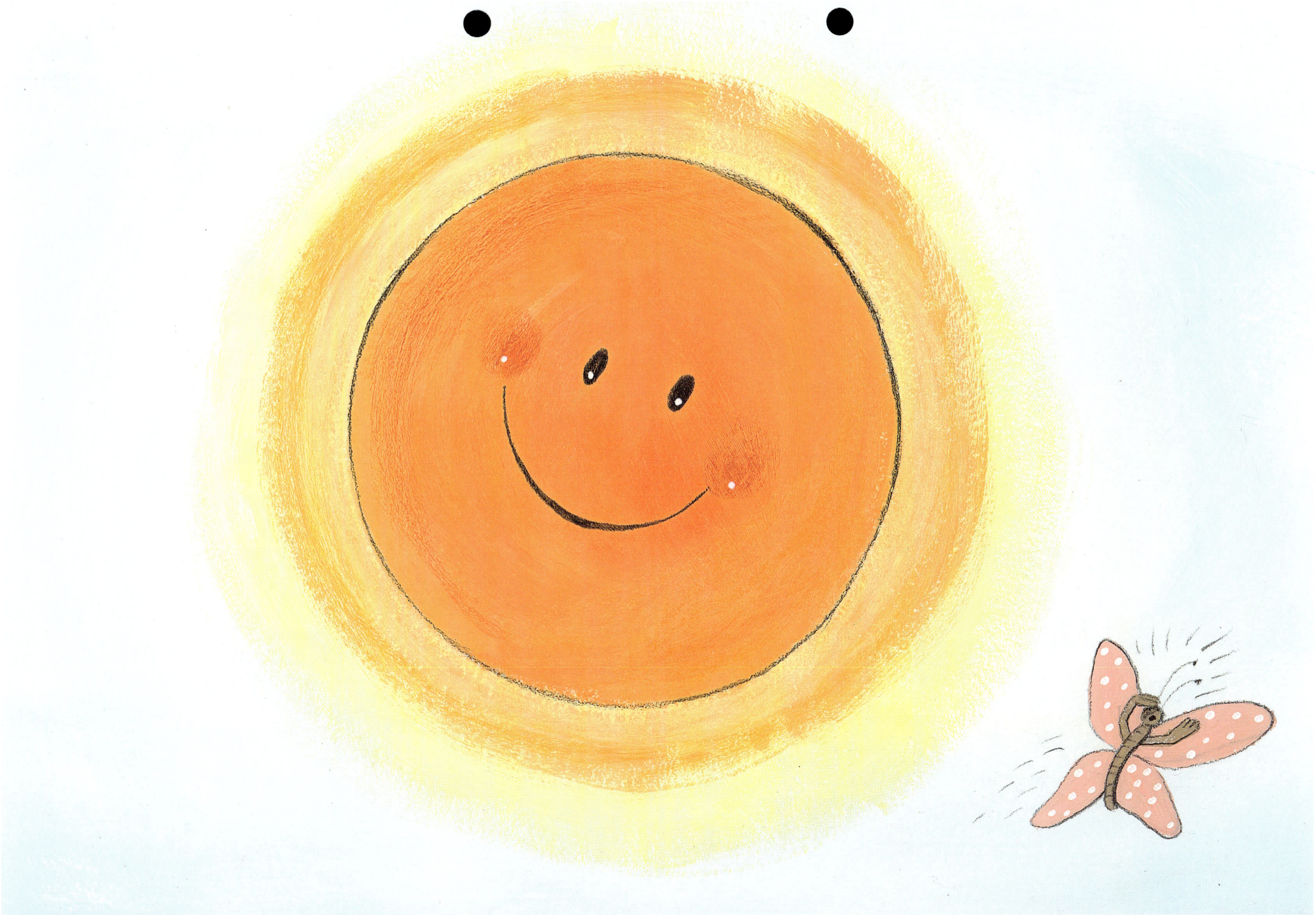

It's warm.

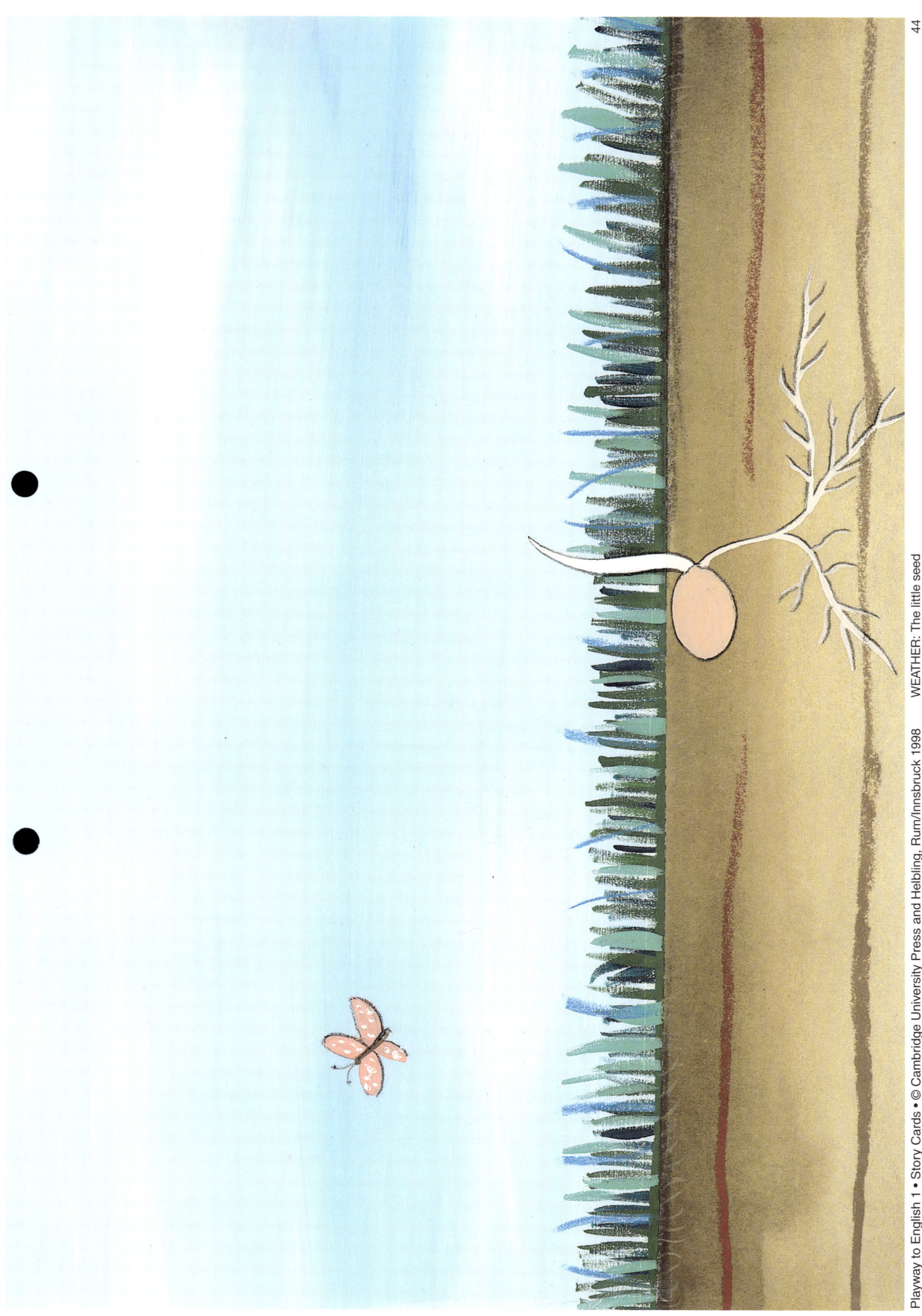

The little seed grows and grows.

●

●

It grows and grows.

●

●

Aaaah! Look at the wonderful flower.

●

●

The lion is ill.

The elephant wants to help.

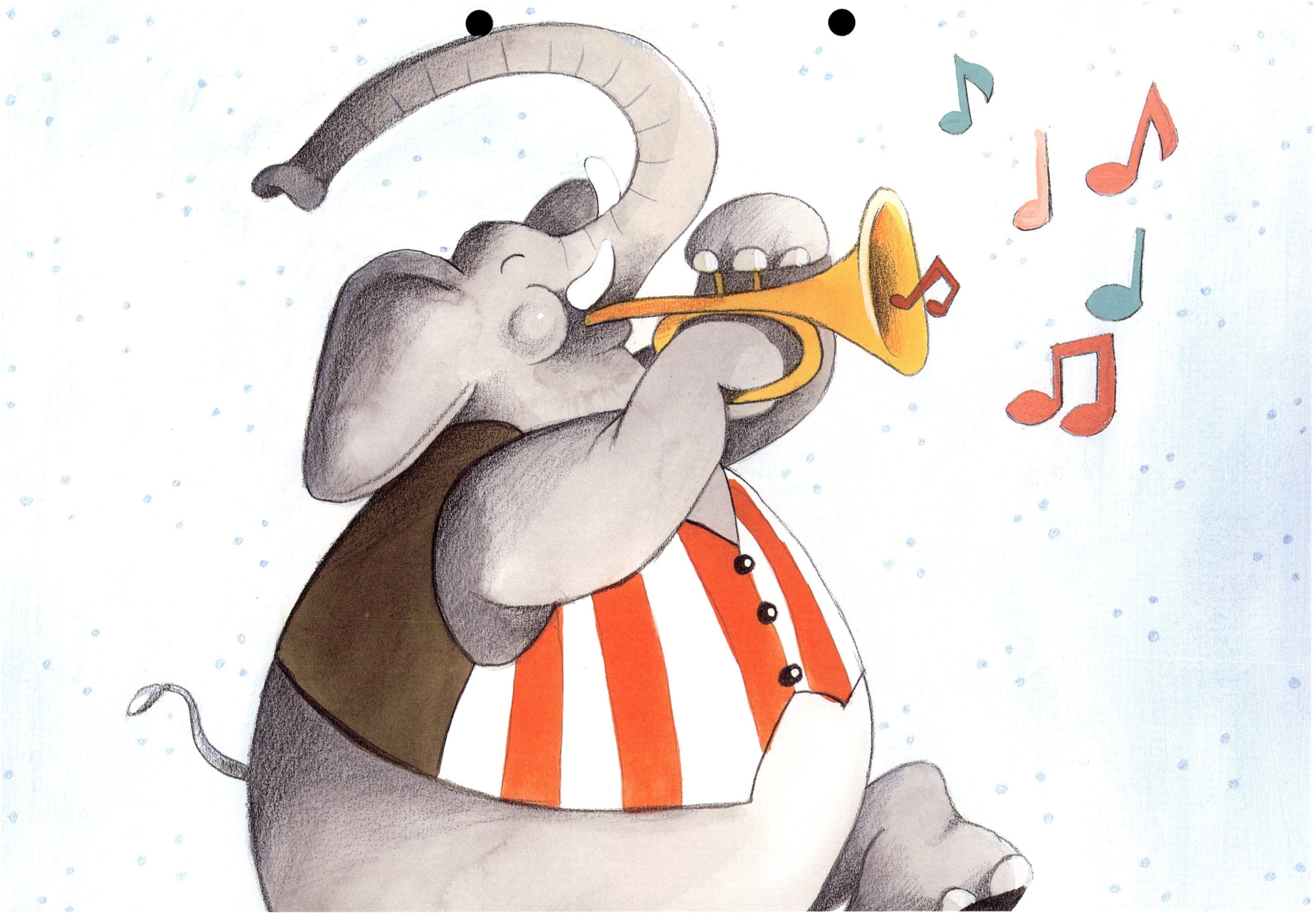

"Lion, listen to my music."

"Stop it, please."

The hippo wants to help.

Playway to English 1 • Story Cards • © Cambridge University Press and Helbling, Rum/Innsbruck 1998

"Lion, listen to my music."

"Stop it, please."

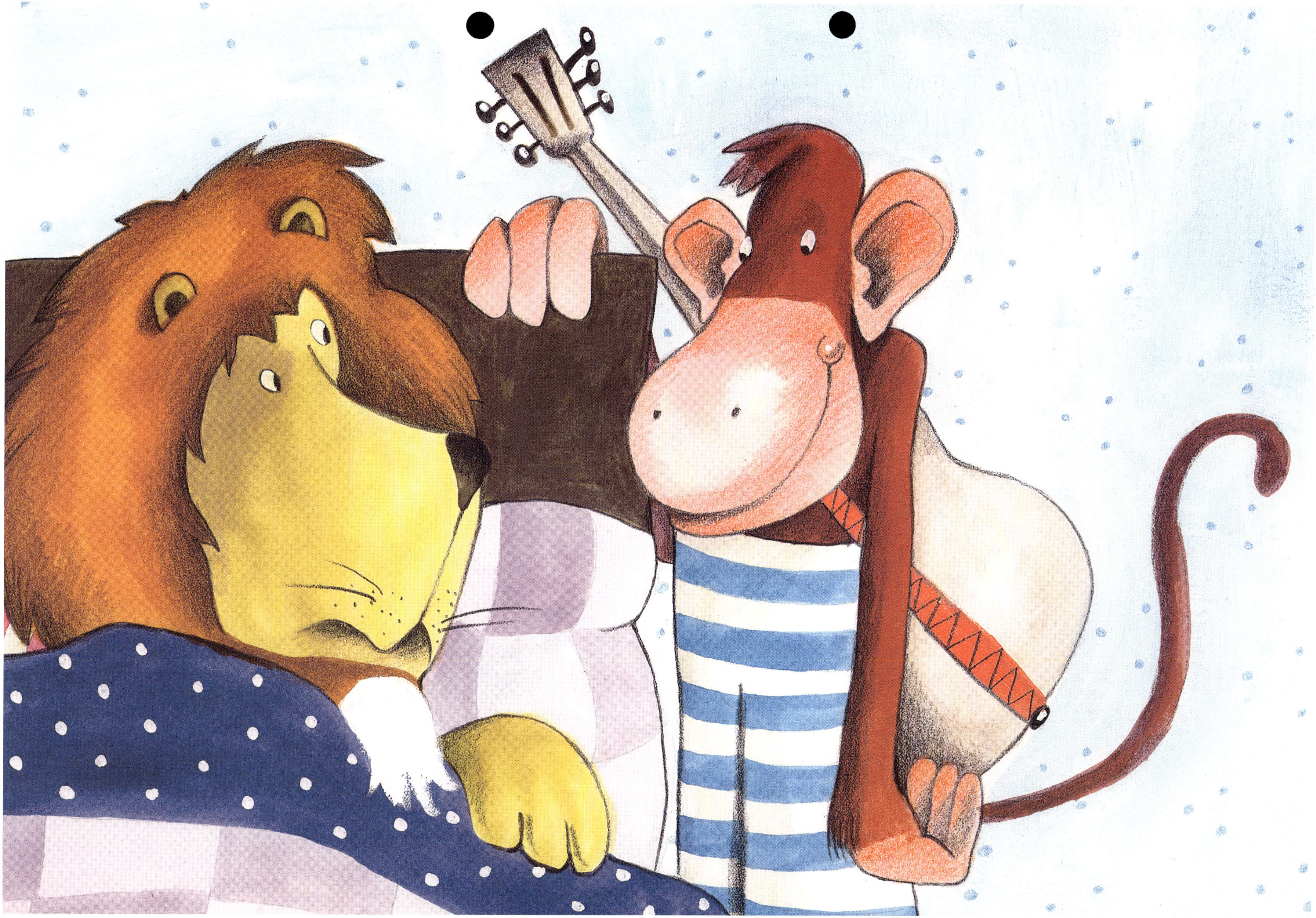

The monkey wants to help.

●

●

"Lion, listen to my music."

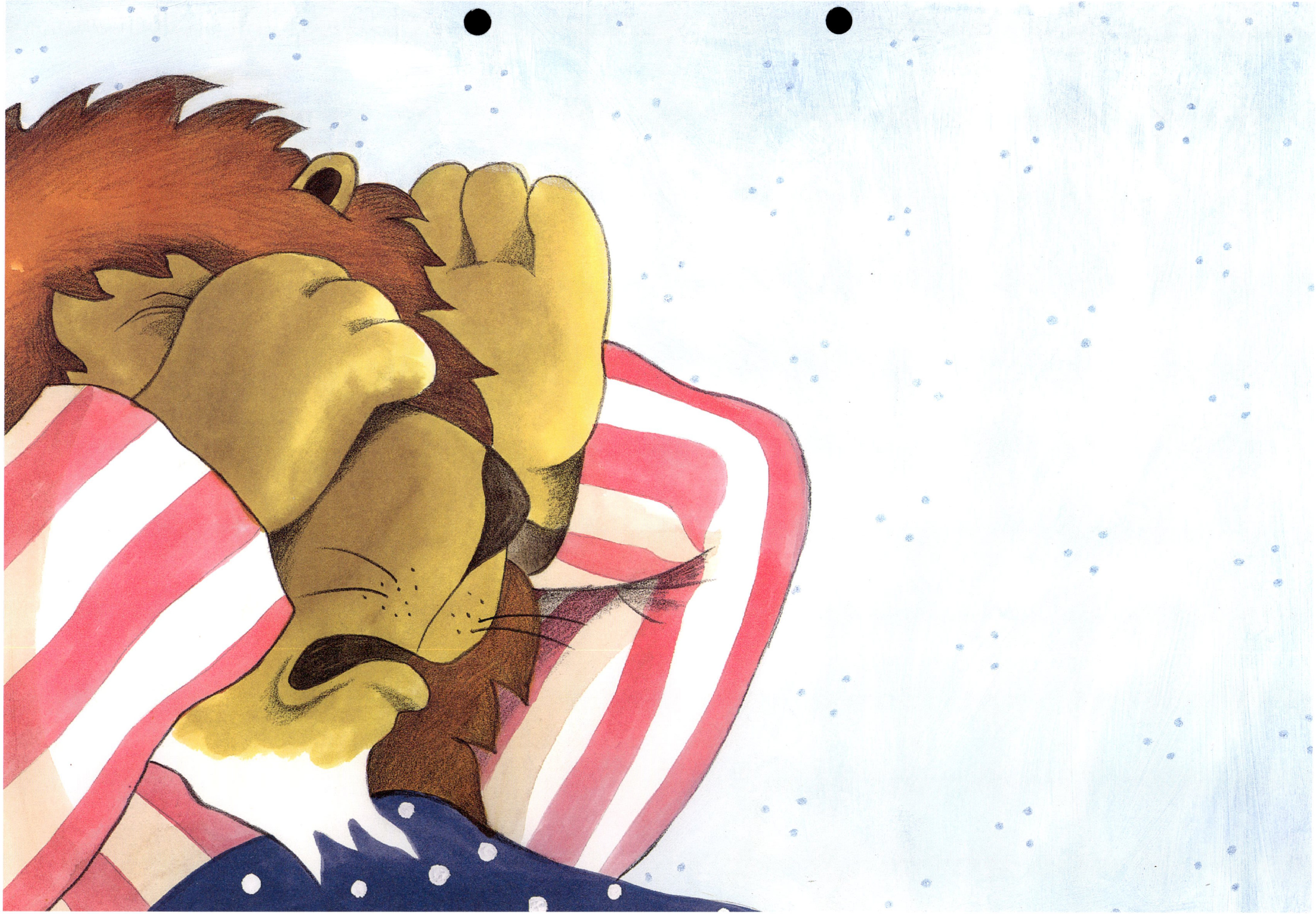

Playway to English 1 • Story Cards • © Cambridge University Press and Helbling, Rum/Innsbruck 1998

"Stop it, please."

●

●

The snake wants to help.

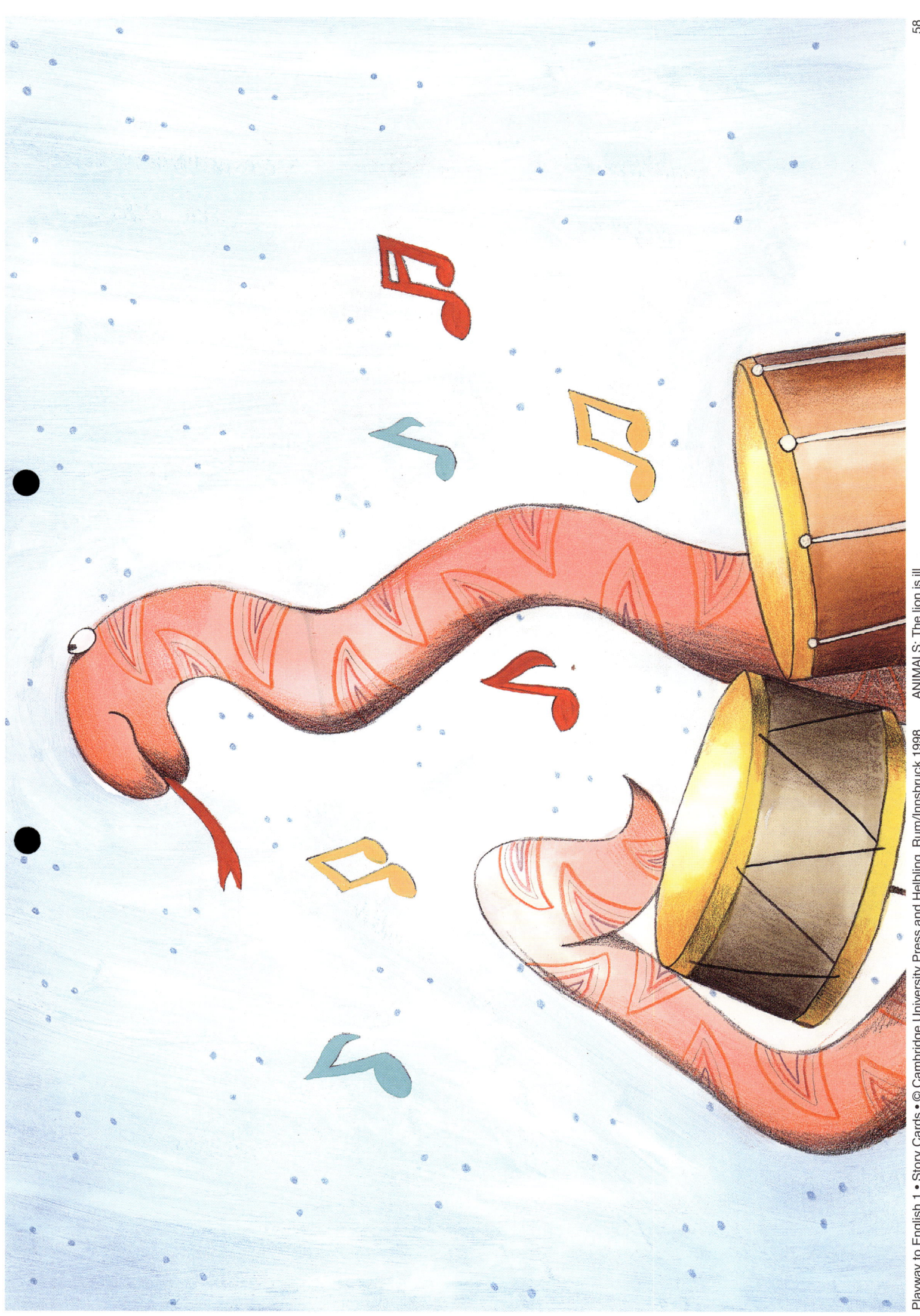

"Lion, listen to my music."

"Stop it, please."

"What's this?"

It's the elephant, the hippo,
the monkey and the snake.

●

●

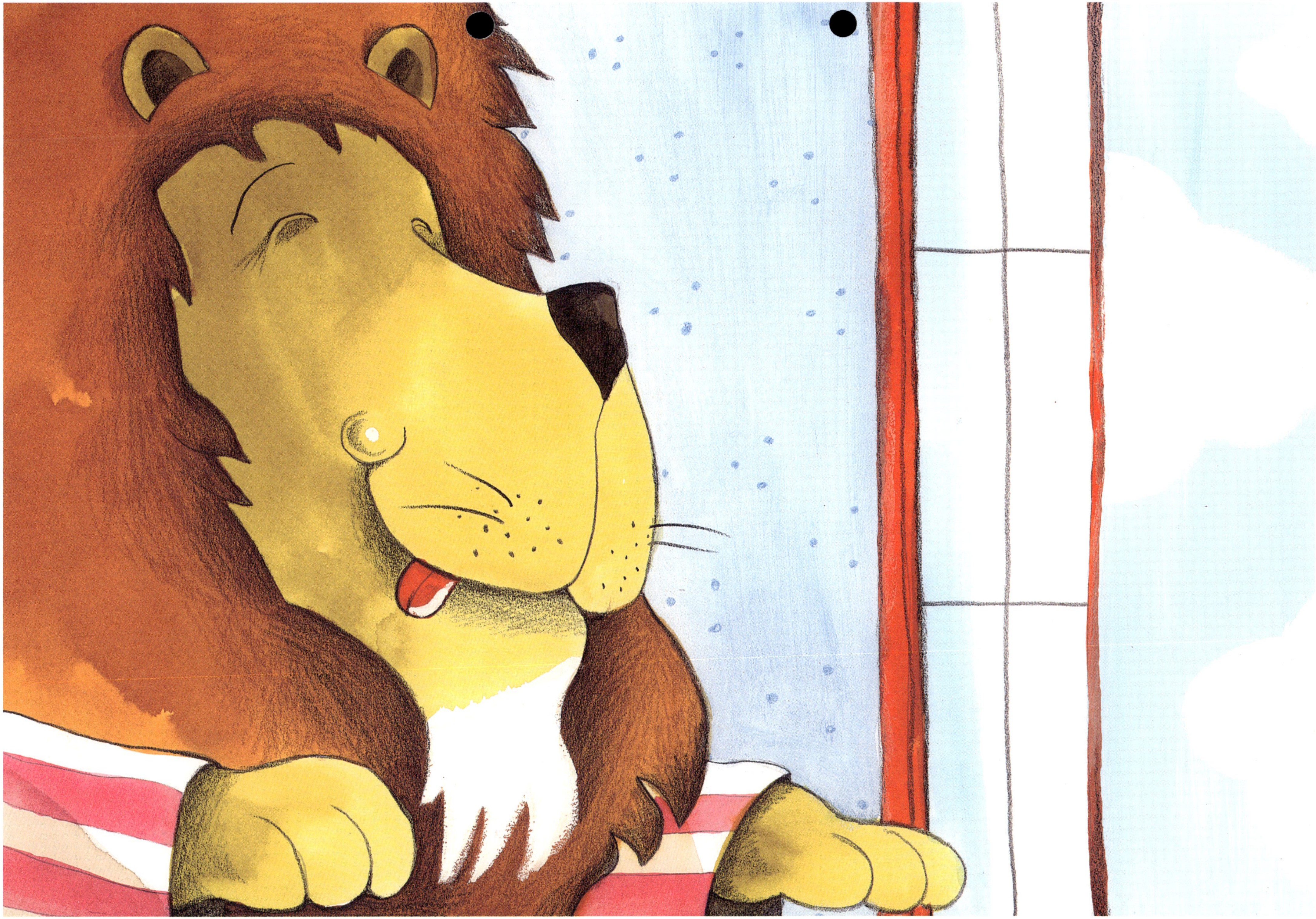

"Oh, thank you for the
wonderful music.
Thank you."

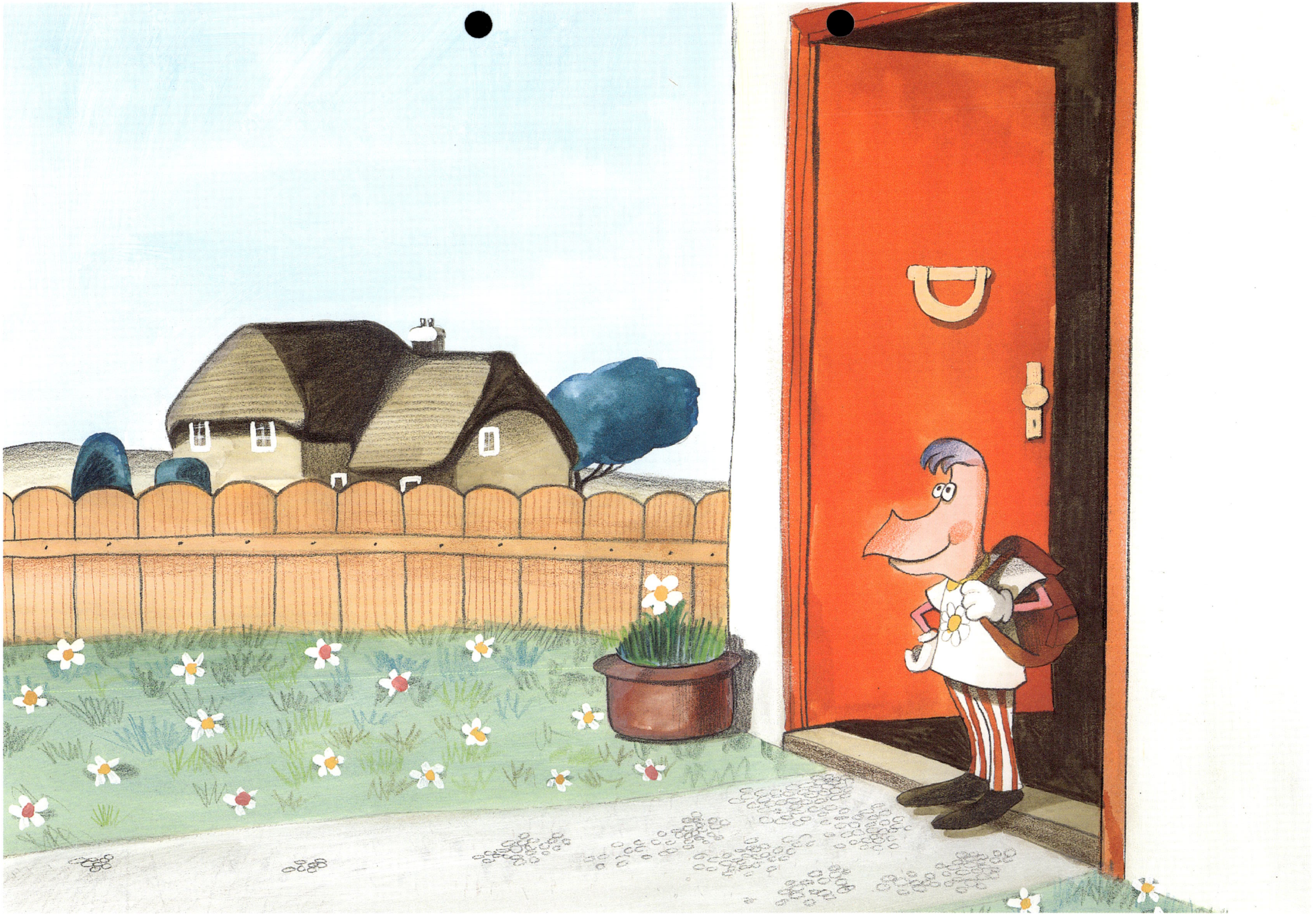

It's summer.
Max goes on holiday.

Playway to English 1 • Story Cards • © Cambridge University Press and Helbling, Rum/Innsbruck 1998

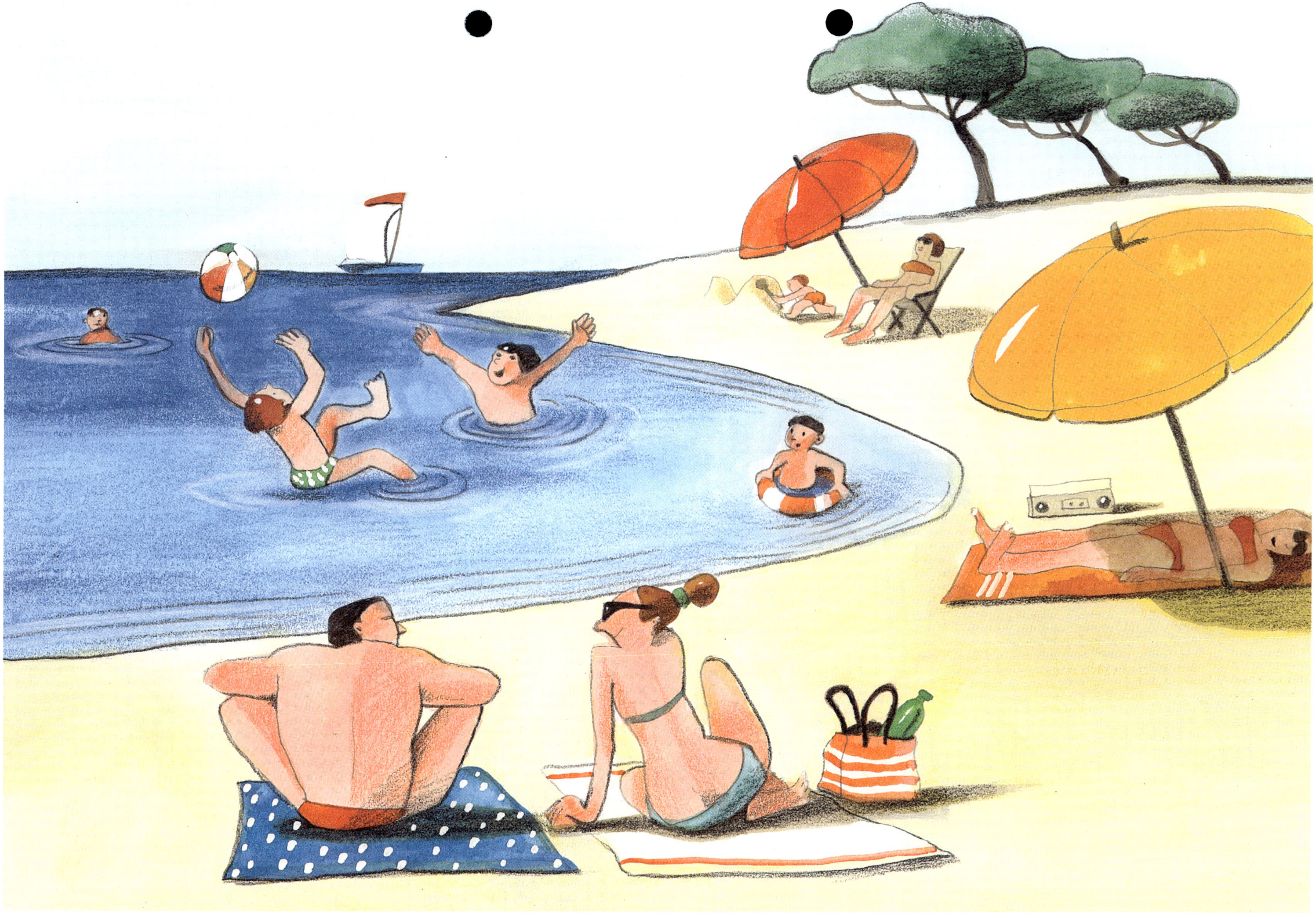

Is Max on the beach?

No.

●

●

Is Max in the jungle?
No.

Is Max in the mountains?
No.

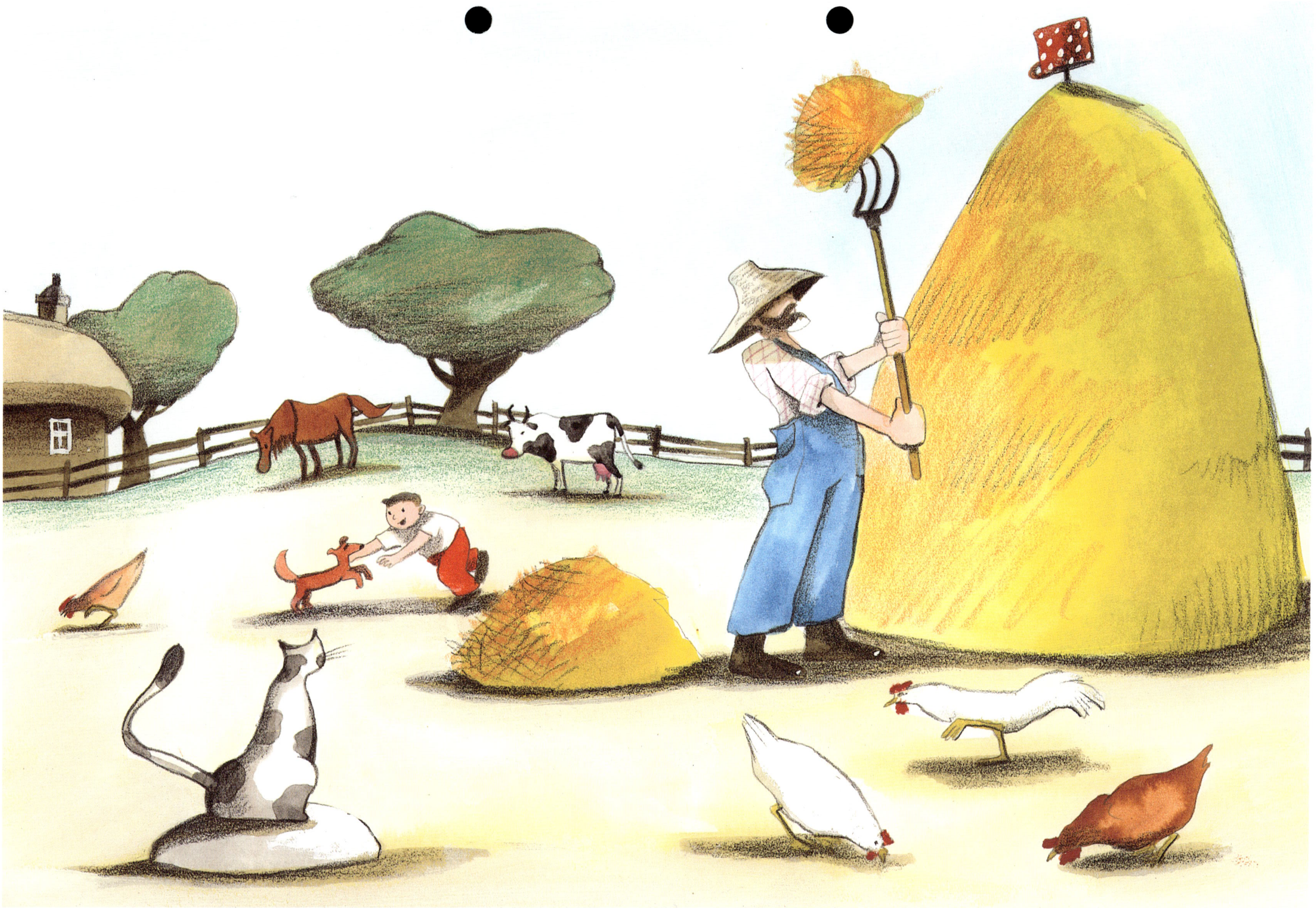

Is Max on the farm?
No.

●

●

Playway to English 1 • Story Cards • © Cambridge University Press and Helbling, Rum/Innsbruck 1998

Is Max in the city?
No.

●

●

Playway to English 1 • Story Cards • © Cambridge University Press and Helbling, Rum/Innsbruck 1998

So, where is Max?
He is not on the beach,
he's not in the jungle,
he's not in the mountains,
he's not on the farm,
and he's not in the city.
So where is he?

Playway to English 1 • Story Cards • © Cambridge University Press and Helbling, Rum/Innsbruck 1998

Look, here he is.
Max is in his garden.

He's eating flowers.
"Yummy."

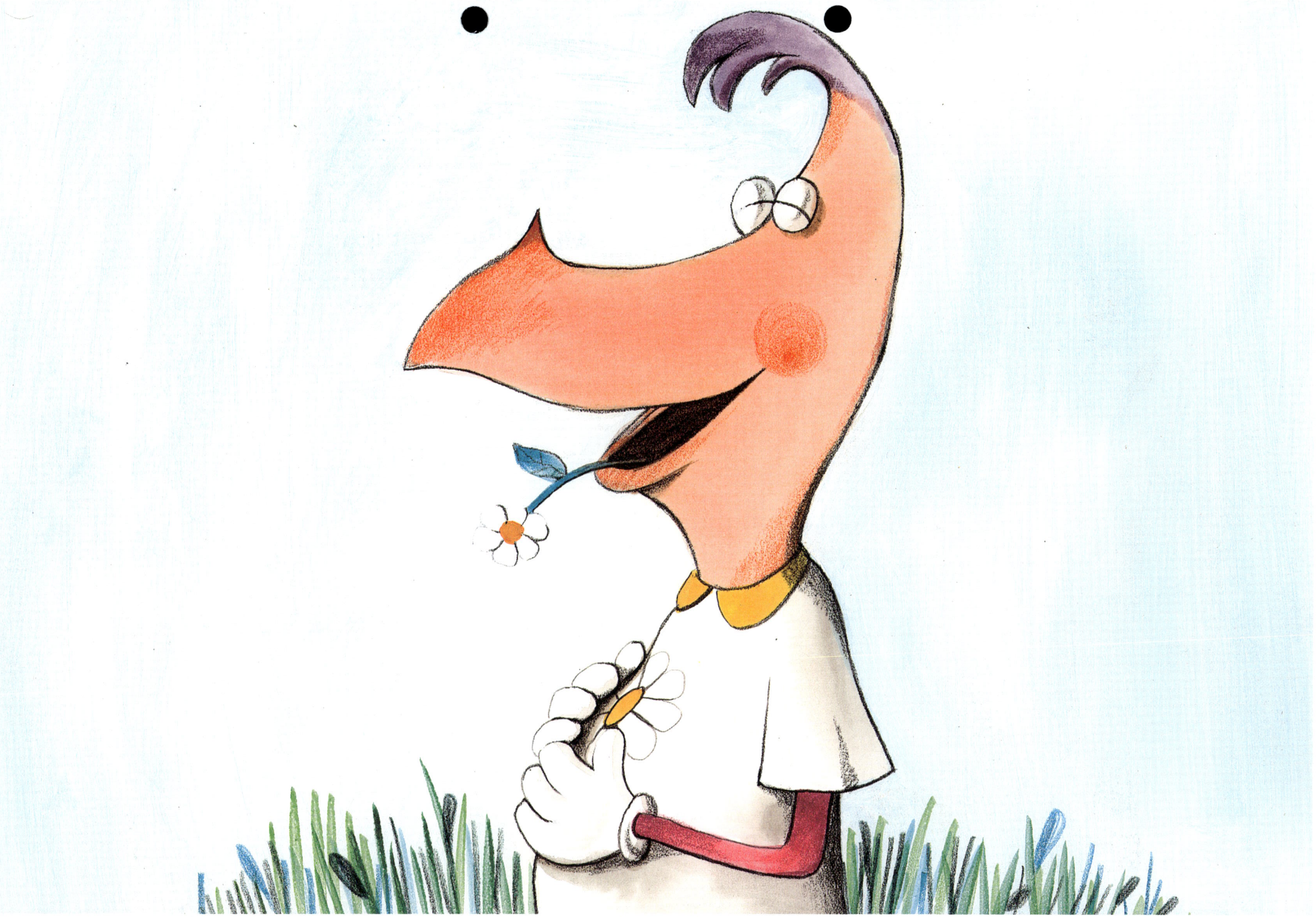

Max is happy.

Playway to English 1 • Story Cards • © Cambridge University Press and Helbling, Rum/Innsbruck 1998

It's Christmas.

Linda, Benny and Max are asleep.

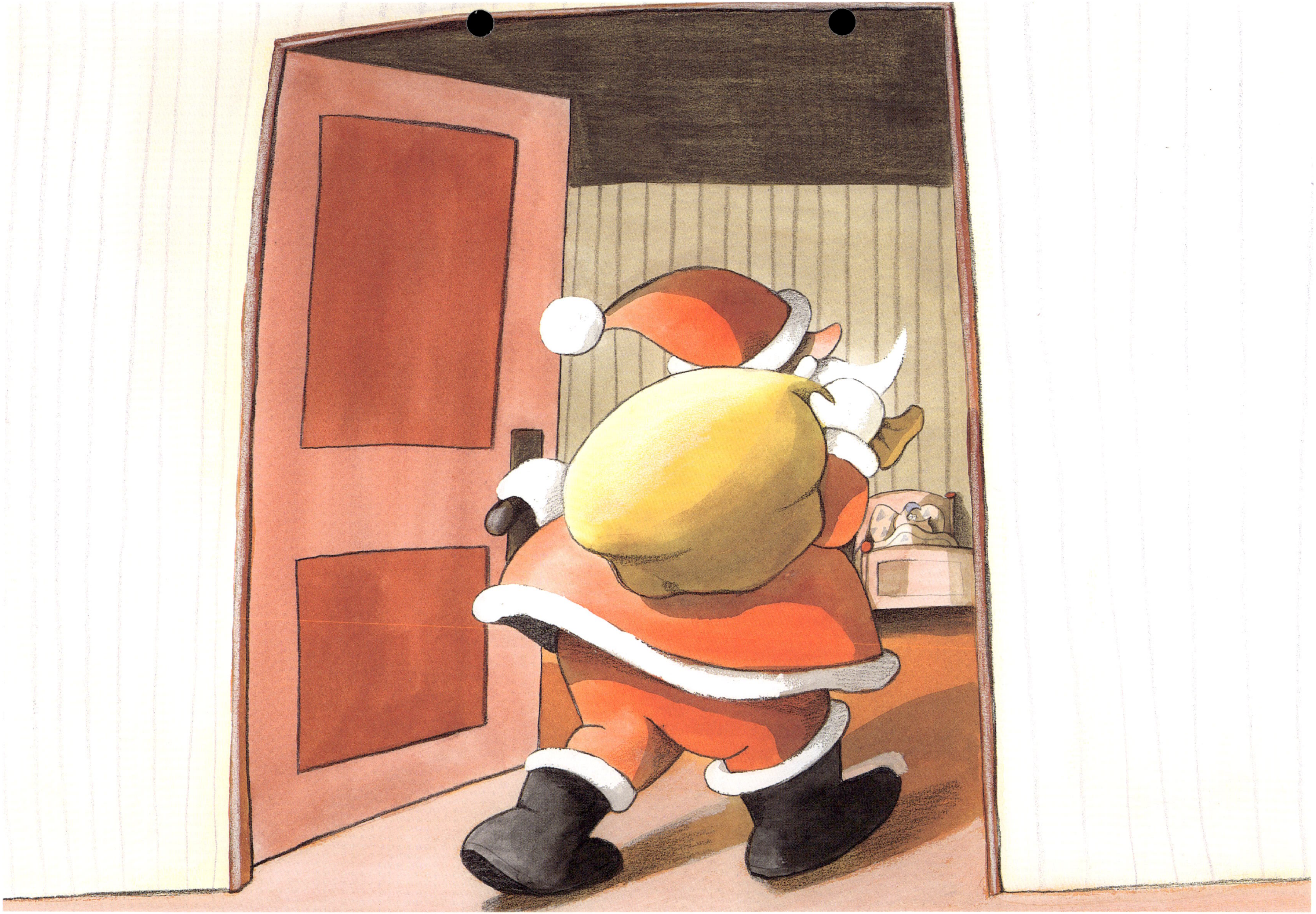

Listen.
It's Father Christmas.

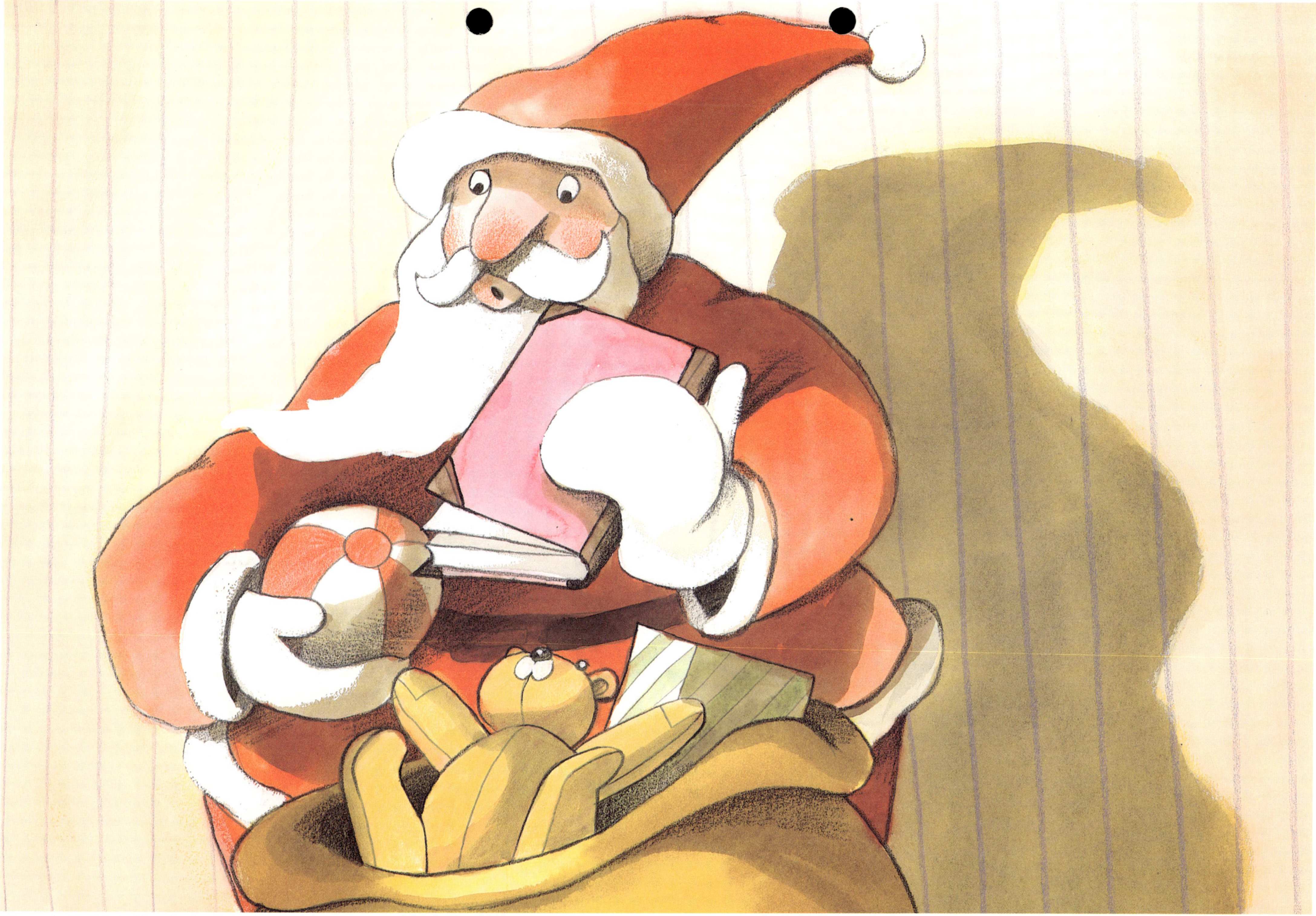

Look! A book for Linda,
a ball for Benny and
a teddy bear for Max.

"One, two, three.
One, two, ... "

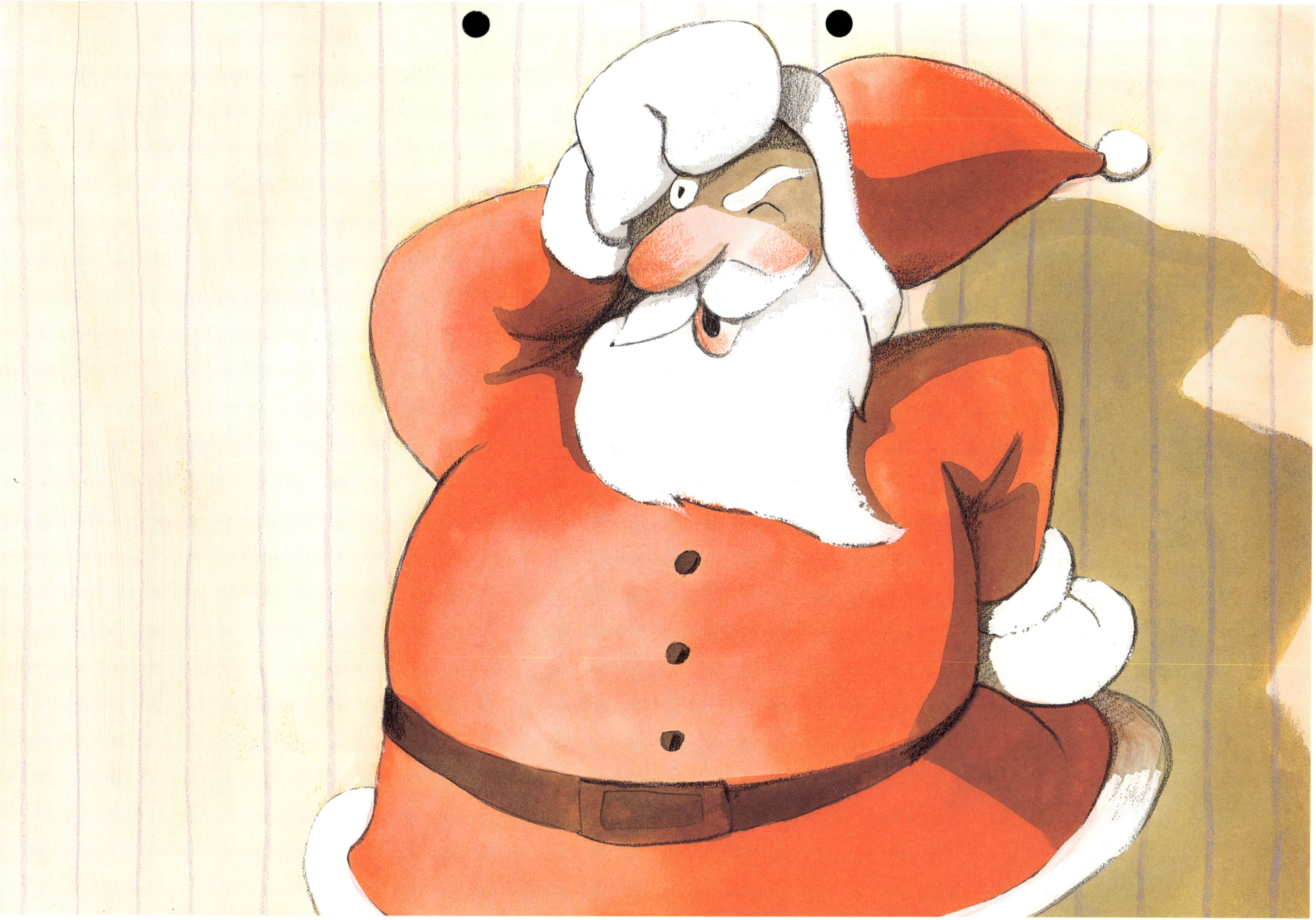

”What can I do?”

Playway to English 1 • Story Cards • © Cambridge University Press and Helbling, Rum/Innsbruck 1998

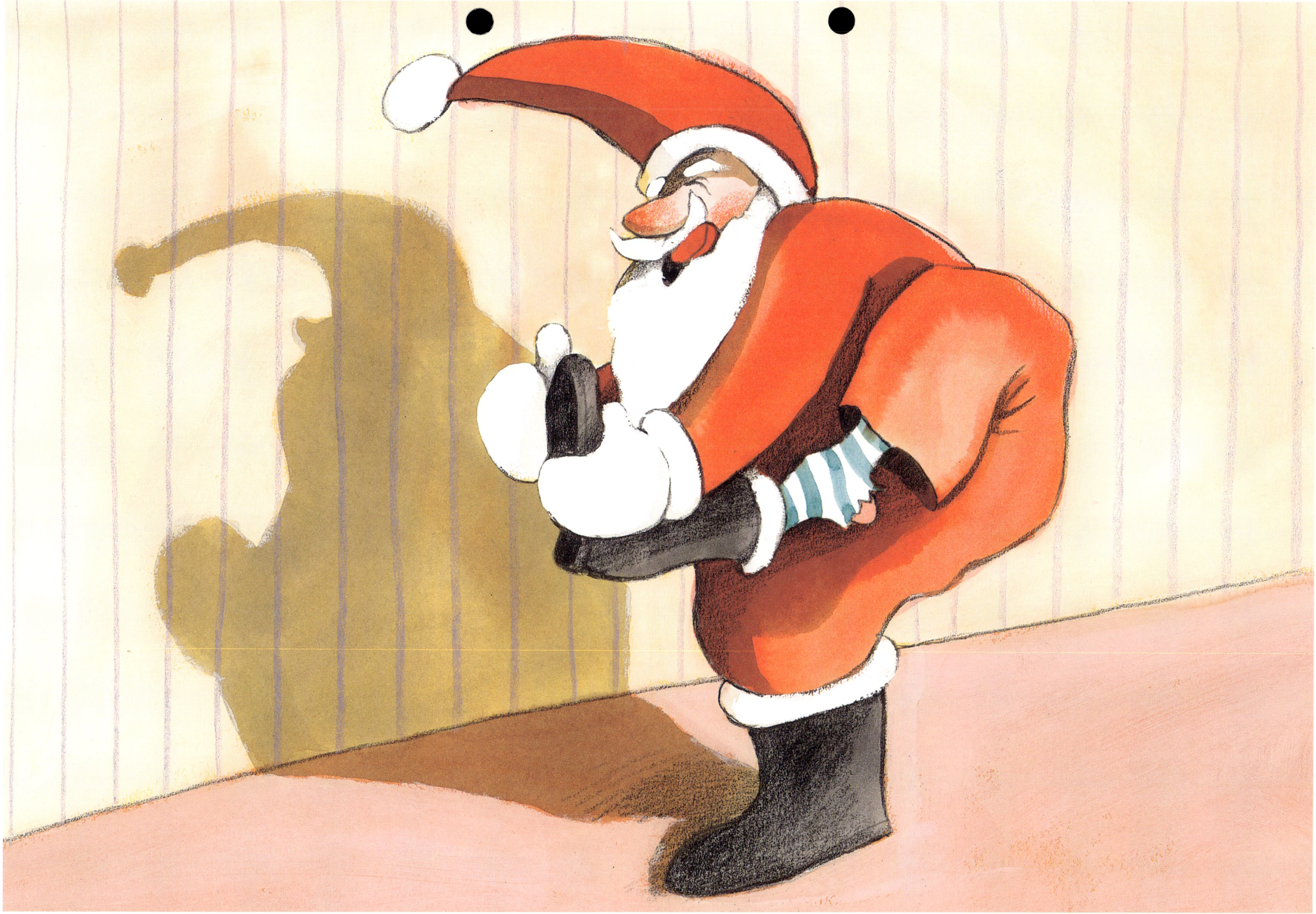

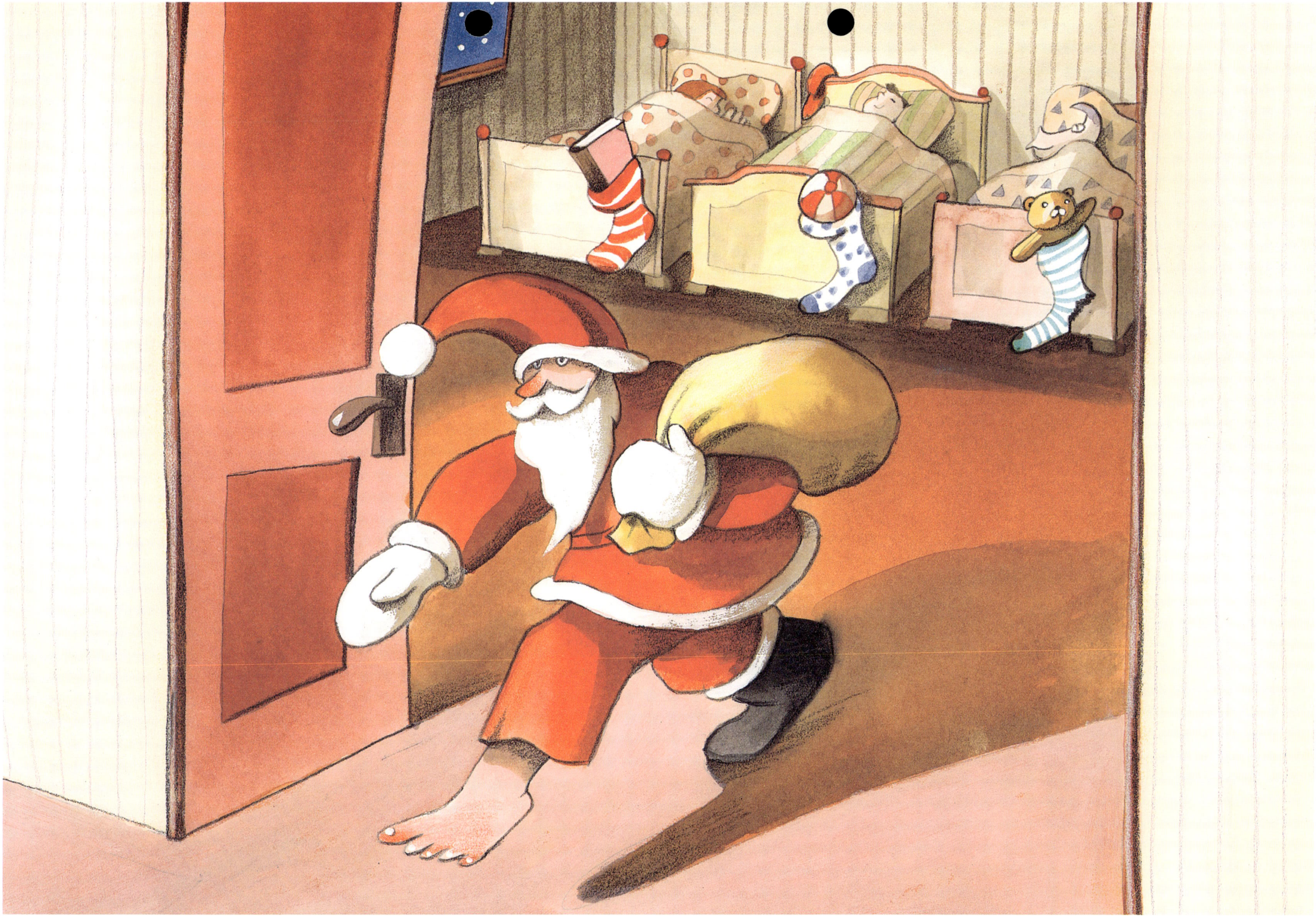

"Brrr. It's cold."

PLAYWAY TO ENGLISH

is a four-level course for teaching English to very young children from beginner level upwards.

PLAYWAY TO ENGLISH uses the SMILE approach:

Skill-oriented learning
Multi-sensory learner motivation
Intelligence building activities
Long-term memory storage of the language through music, movement, rhythm and rhyme
Exciting sketches, stories and games

Children learn to use English confidently through listening and speaking, before they are taught to read and write.

PLAYWAY TO ENGLISH 1 – components

- **Pupil's Book**
  contains colourful pages with varied tasks, including stick-in pictures and puzzle pieces used by the pupils to reconstruct picture stories after viewing cartoon stories on video (or listening to them on cassette/CD if video is not available).

- **Teacher's Guide**
  teacher-friendly lesson plans with complete step-by-step instructions, photocopiable pages and an introduction to the SMILE approach.

- **Picture Cards**
  82 colourful visuals for vocabulary presentation and practice.

- **Story Cards**
  80 A4-size cards, used by the children to reconstruct each cartoon story after viewing it on video (or listening to it on cassette/CD).

- **Class Audio Cassette or CD**
  contains all the stories, chants, rhymes and songs.

- **Stories Video**
  lively sketches performed by puppets, and exciting cartoon stories, serve as reinforcement for the language taught.

- **Stories Audio Cassette or CD**
  the soundtrack of the Stories Video, to be used together with the Story Cards, for situations where video is not available.

- **Activity Book**
  offers a variety of exercises designed to consolidate the language the children have learnt.

- **Activity Book Audio Cassette or CD**
  contains all the texts for the listening tasks in the Activity Book.

- **Max, the glove puppet**
  interacts with the children, making communicating in English fun.

CAMBRIDGE
UNIVERSITY PRESS

Helbling

ISBN 0-521-65691-5

9 780521 656917 >